INFORMATION AND COMPUTER ETHICS

INFORMATION AND COMPUTER ETHICS

Jocelyn O. Padallan

ARCLER
PRESS

www.arclerpress.com

Information and Computer Ethics

Jocelyn O. Padallan

Arcler Press
2010 Winston Park Drive,
2nd Floor
Oakville, ON L6H 5R7
Canada
www.arclerpress.com
Tel: 001-289-291-7705
001-905-616-2116
Fax: 001-289-291-7601
Email: orders@arclereducation.com

ISBN: 978-1-77407-197-7 (Hardcover)

ABOUT THE AUTHOR

Jocelyn O. Padallan is currently pursuing her Master of Science in Information Technology from Laguna State Polytechnic University, Philippines and has Master of Arts in Educational Management from the same University. She has passion for teaching and has been an Instructor at Laguna State Polytechnic, Los Banos Campus, Philippines.

TABLE OF CONTENTS

LIST OF FIGURES

LIST OF TABLES

LIST OF ABBREVIATIONS

ACM	Association for Computing Machinery
AES	advanced encryption standard
AI	artificial intelligence
AITP	Association of Information Technology Professionals
ALA	American Library Association
ALife	artificial life
ALISE	Association for Library and Information Science Education
APTs	advanced persistent threats
ASIST	Association for Information Science and Technology
ASME	American Society for Mechanical Engineers
CEPE	computer ethics: philosophical inquiry series of conferences
CO_2	carbon dioxide
EDT	electronic disturbance theater
GRU	Russian intelligence services
ICBM	intercontinental ballistic missiles
ICCP	Institute for Certification of IT Professionals
ICIE	International Center for Information Ethics
ICTs	information and communication technologies
IDSs	intrusion detection systems
IE	information ethics
IEEE	Institute of Electrical and Electronic Engineers
IPSs	intrusion prevention systems
IT	information technology
NCCV	National Conference on Computing and Values
NSPE	National Society of Professional Engineers

PAPA	Privacy, Accuracy, Property, and Accessibility
SEERI	Software Engineering Ethics Research Institute
SIGCAS	Special Interest Group on Computing and Society
SSL	secure sockets layer
UAV	unmanned aerial vehicle
VSD	value sensitive design
WPI	Worcester Polytechnic Institute

PREFACE

The aim of the book

The ethical issues in the ever-expanding world of technology are being noted with concern and this book aims at spreading the message of ethical use of the informational technology in all its dimensions.

Why a "Handbook of Information and Computer Ethics"?

Digitalization and its sporadic growth in various spheres are perhaps one of the biggest boons of the twentieth century. No sphere in life remains untouched by this advent. However, as the digital world expands, it brings with it an added number of threats which make it incumbent for the users to constantly bear in mind the ethical perspectives of the vast amounts of information available. Ethics is the cornerstone in the entire workplace and this becomes all the more relevant in the digital world. Whereas it is essential to follow the ethical norms whilst exploring the digital world, it is becoming the main area of concern when one uses or designs information on a digital platform. This book caters for the ethical requirements that need to be borne in mind while working on digital technology.

It is essential for all users of IT to be thoroughly familiar with the concepts of information ethics and as to how this knowledge can better arm them while they utilize this important source of information in its myriad forms. It is important to understand the relationship between ethics and information technology and be familiar with the development of computer ethics.

This book covers the important aspect of moral technology with respect to computer ethics along with an understanding of the moral challenges that are paramount while developing IT systems and other technologies including robots and virtual games. The normative theories of computer ethics find a detailed discussion in the book whereby it deals with the various branches of ethics as also how information technology gets affected by globalization.

The digital world cannot remain immune to the criminal activities of the current times. The book takes a look at activities like plagiarism, hacking and cybercrime that have become rampant in this field. The international standards lay down to deal with the challenges facing the ethical concerns in the development of informational technology form an important part of the book. One man's morals may be another man's norms. The book brings out the ethical dilemmas faced by the designers of information technology.

Cyber space cannot remain immune from the conflicts of the nations. The book explores these and talks about the various existing ACM code of ethics that the IT professionals need to follow while designing international codes and software. The requirement for a legal framework to ensure that information technology is morally ethically correct and binding finds a detailed discussion in the book.

A large number of autonomous bodies have made a foray into the social media channels and have gone on to strengthen their presence. The book delves upon the need for these channels to be diligent and follow the ethical codes while dealing with the data of their users. The book covers the various challenges faced in implementation of the regulations that exist and culminates with providing information on the existing malicious software that can pose a challenge to the user. The handbook shall be beneficial equally to novices and experts in the field as it guides them through the sensitive issue of morals and ethics involved in the optimum and efficient use of IT.

1

Introduction to Information Ethics

CONTENTS

Information ethics (IE) is that branch of ethics which outlines the connection between the collection, organization, and use of information with the ethical standards and moral codes that govern the conduct of an individual in the society. The chapter talks about information as a resource ethic with respect to the product ethics of information sector. It also highlights the development of computer ethics which has now become essential for every individual to understand. Professional computer ethics have also been discussed in this chapter, which would help readers to understand the importance of being ethical in the professional world.

1.1. INTRODUCTION

In common parlance and professional context, all written works on ethics present an incomprehensible range of insinuations and implications. Ethics and morals are two terms that are often used in place of each other. This is because the distinction between them is ambiguous. Morality describes customs, ideals, and principles, that define and bring about a change in the society and guides an individual or community to differentiate right from wrong. The language of ethics is how we translate these values and principles in our conversations.

Aristotle was the forerunner in establishing ethics as an indispensable aspect of morality. He founded ethics as an academic discipline. Rafael Capurro, the head of International Center for Information Ethics (ICIE), is of the opinion:

"As self-referential process ethics is an unending quest on explicit and implicit use of the moral code that is to say of respect or disrespect, with regard to individual and social communication. In other words, ethics observes the ways we communicate with each other as moral persons and the ways this moral identity is understood. There is, indeed, no unbiased, ethical observer."

Information and communication technologies (ICTs) have overwhelmingly altered many facets of life, including the nature of entertainment, work, communication, education, health care, manufacturing, business, social relations, and conflict. ICTs have had, and continue to have, unfathomable, and profound impact on our moral lives and on present-day ethical debates (Floridi, 2006). A fundamental change can be seen, over the last decade, in the dissertation of experts in the field of information science.

The point of focus has shifted from a primary concern with technique (which includes topics like acquisitions and moving through cataloging and conservation to user education and beyond), towards other diverse issues in which the ethical dimension is more dominating (intellectual property, user privacy, and serving the socially excluded)

The last decade has witnessed a rudimentary change, in the desertions of specialists, in the field of information science. The focus of this chapter has shifted from a predominant concern with technique to an engagement with a range of issues in which there is an ethical dilemma involved. By techniques, we mean topics like acquisition, cataloging, and conserving to user education and much more than that. The range of issues that is the primary concern are intellectual property, user privacy, and catering to all strata of the society.

Only a critical examination of information science literature will reveal if this suggestion holds true or not. The evaluation would be a challenging task given that the majority of the professional conversations, be it written, spoken or electronic, is very technical and is not expected to change in the near future. The literature of theory still sets out to discuss information as a scientific phenomenon, rather than a product of moral action.

It is vital to analyses implicit values from different perspectives and standpoints before formulating and executing information policies. Capurro reiterates "As a self-referential process ethics is an unending quest on explicit and implicit use of the moral code that is to say of respect or disrespect, with regard to individual and social communication. There is, indeed, no unbiased, ethical observer."

Berghtol worked on an ethical warrant and stressed on how crucial it is to understand the context. She discussed about "cultural hospitality" which forms the basis for the ethical knowledge of organization systems. Cultural hospitality also aids in representing new organization systems and update the existing knowledge systems and the various ethnicities to which the individuals belong.

It was during the Second World War that IE got recognition in the academics. This academic field was not planned but was born inadvertently. Norbert Wiener, a philosopher, and a scientist, were working in collaboration on some cutting-edge technologies including the invention of digital computers and radar. They were also working on a novel antiaircraft cannon with the following features:

- The aircraft could detect the presence of an airplane;

- It could collect are necessary data about the airplane like its speed and flight path;
- It could envisage what position the airplane would in a few seconds;
- It could estimate the target and calculate where to fire;
- It could have decision-making skills.

The actions were to take place almost immediately and that too without human involvement. Weiner had extraordinary insight and foresight. He had the foresight to realize that the new inventions in the field of science and technology that he and his colleagues were working on would have "enormous potential for good and for evil."

Weiner prophesied that the post-war period would be characterized by a significant presence of information technology (IT) in every aspect of life. The change would be as profound as the post-Industrial Revolution era in the nineteenth and early twentieth century. Weiner also foretold that new moral conflicts and opportunities would arise as a result of the second industrial revolution. This could be termed as the "automatic age."

In the current age, "IE" has been interpreted by different researchers working in fields like business ethics, information science, computer science, medical ethics, social epistemology and computer ethics in various ways. This Babel was inevitable considering that this is a new field and information is diverse in nature. The detailed scope and nature of IE have, unfortunately, caused some confusion. This situation could quickly be resolved with the help of a unified approach that can help to explain and relate the main senses in which IE has been discussed.

1.2. INFORMATION AS A RESOURCE ETHIC

IE was a broad term, in the 1980s, to discuss issues pertaining to information (or data) confidentiality, reliability, quality, and usage.

Information Society is a social order where economic and cultural activities are mostly comprised of creation, distribution, and manipulation of information. The emergence of information societies can be attributed to the advancement in the field of ICTs. The advent of information society has been characterized by fundamental moral challenges. The intricacies of these challenges are multiplying exponentially.

The most urgent need of the hour is to have an IE structure in place that can bring infosphere into existence. Infosphere is an environment which is populated by information, knowledge, and data as well as their related lifecycle activities like conception, distribution, security, storage, and obliteration after their intended use, etc. Mankind is expected to thrive in this new environment.

The purpose of having IE is to identify and resolve technical complexities that may arise in this new environment.

This field is new, and the problem it poses is also compelling. Also, the concept of information and its related phenomena are multifaceted.

The Earth is a dynamic planet, and it has undergone different stages of expansion, diminution, and globalization ever since it came into existence. This present era of globalization is apparently here to stay because it has been accompanied by phenomenal changes in transportation and communication all over the globe (Brandt and Henning, 2002).

The most notable feature of this era is the rapid movement of bytes and atoms. This movement has been inexpensive, dependable, constant, and universal since the last decade. This has resulted in short turnaround times for economic transactions, financial exchanges, social relations, movement of information and so on. The omnipresence of information has shrunk physical environment and human life.

1.2.1. Resource Perspective

From a "resource" perspective, the moral machine needs abundant information to function accurately. TO consider information solely as a resource restricts the scope of its analysis. It is essential to exercise caution so that all ethical discourse is not reduced to the nuances of higher quantity, quality, and intelligibility of informational resources. It cannot always be claimed more is better. Removal of information (sometimes obvious and conscious) can often make a substantial difference.

Whether the (quantitative and qualitative) presence or the (total) absence of information-as-a-resource is in question, it is obvious that there is a perfectly reasonable sense in which IE may be described as the study of the moral issues arising from "the triple-A" of informational resources. The triple-A are:

- Availability: Presence of information;
- Accuracy: Correctness of information; and

- Accessibility: Convenience in obtaining information.

The study of IE has to be independent of its physical support and format. IE from resource perspective has to address other issues as well like the 'digital divide,' the challenge of information glut and evaluating whether a source of information is authentic and can be relied on.

1.2.2. The Product Ethics of Information Sector

IE is based on the premise that information may be considered as a product. Ethics encompasses moral issues that surface in the context of legislation misinformation, accountability, propaganda, advertising, plagiarism, testimony, and liability among others and more generally of pragmatic rules of communication à la Grice. Kant's analysis of the immorality of lying is one of the best-known case studies in the philosophical literature concerning this kind of IE.

A classic example of how improper management of information can have disastrous results can be understood by studying the case of Trojan War where Laocoon and Cassandra were not successful in ensuring that the Trojans exercised proper caution against the Greeks.

"What is right?" and "What is wrong?" has been a pressing question for human beings for centuries. In their everyday life, differentiating right from wrong has been challenging for almost every man and woman. The outcome of this has been endless debates, conflict of opinions, deliberations, and arguments. These discussions have only intensified with the passage of time. The birth of "Information Society" and extraordinary progress in Information and Communications Technologies (ICTs), has added a new chapter in the on-going debate on what is right and what is wrong.

Information professionals now have a huge responsibility to differentiate right from wrong and also determine what is ethical and what is not. It is extremely challenging to determine if an action is ethical or unethical. Informational professionals are burdened with this responsibility, and they are now trying to come up with solutions in numerous ways.

Information has now proliferated in all branches of information. The widespread use of ICT tools and techniques have raised very pertinent points about security, accessibility, right to express, privacy, and other related questions. As a result of this, it is of vital importance for information professionals to resolve all issues related to the ethical use of information and determine new ways to assist their clients in a fair and ethical manner.

1.3. RELATIONSHIP BETWEEN ETHICS AND INFORMATION ETHICS

Ethics often referred to as moral philosophy, is that division of philosophy that is concerned with systematizing, defending, and providing guidance on ethical and unethical conduct. Moral behavior merits doing the right things and taking the right action, irrespective of the situation. However, it is very difficult to decide on what is the right thing to do and what is wrong. Ethics is concerned with providing reasonable justification for our decisions. It evaluates if an action is moral or immoral.

The role of information in routine decision-making and the advancement of our society is significant. The absence of precise and timely information will make it very challenging to make the right choices and decide the course of action. Ethics facilitates in the establishment of a code of conduct that can be applied in particular situations. Ethical principles also aid in setting up standards that can guide information professionals.

The omnipresence of information in all fields of human exertions has given rise to new challenges for the human. The problem now is the presence of an exorbitant amount of information as opposed to the lack of it. In the present situation, it has become extremely difficult to use information judiciously to resolve our routine challenges and decision making.

IE is expected to pave the path for problem-solving and utilizing information productively. IE is concerned with the ethical conduct of the users of information. It reinforces their accountability and obligation. It deals with the moral questions emerging from the use of information and the related activities during its lifecycle including creation, protection, distribution, and possibly destruction.

The task of providing information is not very challenging and tough. There is now abundant ICT tools and techniques at our disposal. The information landscape has evolved into a very intricate and complicated information network. Also, the demand of information users all over the globe have now varied and broadened. These factors have complicated the situation. Hence, there is an additional endeavor, of distributing information to the right person at the right time in the right manner. And this is not an easy task anymore.

One disturbing fact is the presence of 'information divide.' This is a result of inequalities in wealth creation and distribution among the various countries. This has manifested in generation and use of information also.

1.4. NORBERT WIENER'S FOUNDATION OF INFORMATION ETHICS

In 1950, Wiener wrote a book on the probable effects of information technologies. It was called 'The Human Use of Human Beings,' and it covered fundamental human values like wealth, health, contentment, liberty, opportunities, and capabilities. The book is relevant even today. This decade can be called the "Internet Age' and is characterized by the perennial search for "global IE."

The notions and measures suggested by Wiener can be used to recognize, evaluate, and find a solution to all social and ethical dilemmas that have arisen with the emergence of information technologies. These technologies encompass all mediums of information like computer, laptops, television, mobiles, books, and libraries, media, and journalism.

"IE is a very appropriate name for this branch of study founded by Wiener since his philosophy can be applied in all types of information technologies. Computer ethics has emerged from the field of IE that was founded by Wiener. Weiner evaluated many issues in his works many years ago that are pertinent even in the present era (see Wiener 1948, 1950; 1954, 1964):

"Computers and unemployment, computers, and security, computers, and learning, computers for persons with disabilities, computers, and religion, information networks and globalization, virtual communities, teleworking, the responsibilities of computer professionals, the merging of human bodies and machines, 'agent' ethics, artificial intelligence (AI), and a number of other issues" (see Bynum, 2000, 2004, 2005, 2006).

Weiner's work on IE was based on the branch of science referred to as Cybernetics. Cybernetics is concerned with the way human brains and electronic machines work and invent machines that can function like the human brain. Wiener identified "great principles of justice" that all civilizations should adhere to. He formulated a feasible approach to evaluate IE issues and find a solution for the same as and when they occur. Weiner did not intend to establish a new branch. Rather IE was founded incidentally as a branch of academic research.

The field simply emerged from the many ethical remarks and examples that he included in his writings on cybernetics. The term "cybernetics" was derived from the Greek word for the pilot of a ship. Weiner came up with this term for this new branch of science. However, the terms like "IE" and "computer ethics" which subsequently arose from his research.

Although he had published his book, The Human Use of Human Being in 1950, that dealt with the moral and social consequences of cybernetics and electronic computers, Weiner did not call his work an offshoot of applied ethics Neither did he did not describe what he was doing as the creation of a new branch of applied ethics nor did he give an explanation on the purpose of his work.

To understand Wiener's foundation for IE, therefore, we must observe what he does in his works, rather than look for metaphilosophically explanations about his intentions. Weiner's work on human nature focused on the physical anatomy of man and the power of human physiology in facilitating creative actions and opportunities for learning. He provided clarifications about this potential by comparing the physiology of humans and less evolved organisms:

"Cybernetics takes the view that the structure of the machine or of the organism is an index of the performance that may be expected from it. The fact that the mechanical rigidity of the insect is such as to limit its intelligence while the mechanical fluidity of the human being provides for his almost indefinite intellectual expansion is highly relevant to the point of view of this book. Man's advantage over the rest of nature is that he has the physiological and hence the intellectual equipment to adapt himself to radical changes in his environment. The human species is strong only insofar as it takes advantage of the innate, adaptive, learning faculties that its physiological structure makes possible." (Wiener, 1954, pp. 57–58, italics in the original).

1.4.1. Wiener and His Account of a Good Life

According to Wiener, human beings are very intelligent and should exercise their decision-making power to control their own lives and live well. They must have the liberty to engage in innovative and malleable actions, and this should result in maximizing their full potential. This should be the objective of human lives. It is obvious that one person's accomplishment will vary from any other individual's accomplishments. This is because different human beings will have different levels of ability and aptitude.

There is a vast scope to prosper in an enormous number of ways in various fields like being a teacher, nurse, engineer, doctor, accountant, scientist singer, trader, entrepreneur, politician, leader, and so on. This way, it is possible to lead a flourishing human life.

Weiner was of the opinion that that human life should be based on the values and impartiality. This led to the "great principles of justice" which according to Weiner should be the basis for forming a society. Weiner strongly believed that these principles would enable humans to thrive through various flexible actions. Wiener's great principles can be referred to as "The Principle of Freedom," "The Principle of Equality," and "The Principle of Benevolence." Weiner did not coin the names for his principles; he only stated them. The following list of principles can be derived from his work (Figure 1.1).

- **The Principle of Freedom:** In order to establish justice, "the liberty of each human being to develop in his freedom the full measure of the human possibilities embodied in him."
- **The Principle of Equality:** Justice necessitates "the equality by which what is just for A and B remains just when the positions of A and B are interchanged."
- **The principle of Benevolence:** Justice entails "a goodwill between man and man that knows no limits short of those of humanity itself."

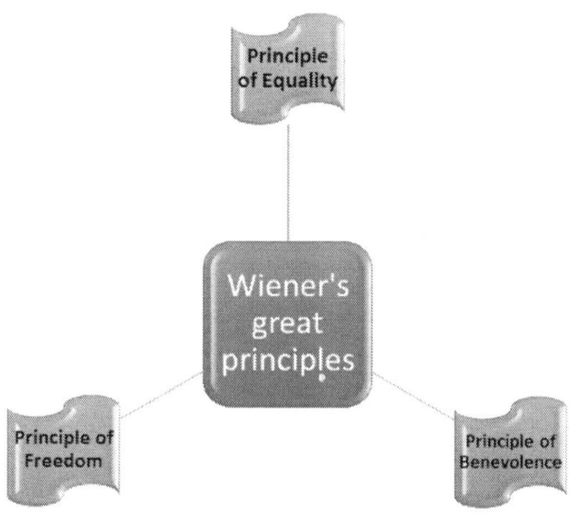

Figure 1.1: Wiener's three great principles of justice in the field of information ethics.

Wieners' works are based on human nature and an ideal society. From his works, we can derive that different cultures that are characterized by various practices, languages, traditions, and religions can provide the required platform for supporting a decent human life. Wiener supported the view that "variety and possibility belong to the very structure of the human organism," hence he could welcome the existence of a broad diversity of cultures in the world to maximize the possibility of choice and creative action.

According to Weiner, a society should support an enabling environment where a man can maximize their potential as sophisticated beings that can process information, make choices and be responsible for their own lives. To establish such a social order, freedom, equality, and human compassion should be there in the society. Ethical relativists opine that there can be no universal foundation for ethics since diverse laws, ethics, and norms exist in the worldwide.

Wiener's response was that as per his work on human life, humans can adopt various cultures and traditions while still observing "the great principles of justice." These principles lay the foundation for ethics across diverse cultures.

1.4.2. Methodology for Information Ethics

An evaluation of Winer's approach to resolving IE issues it can be observed that he attempts to assimilate new cases by applying already existing, ethically acceptable laws, rules, and practices. This is particularly true in the case of his book "The Human Use of Human Beings." All societies have principles, customs, rules, and regulation that collectively mold human conduct in that society.

According to Moor, these policies constitute a "received policy cluster." In a reasonably unbiased society, they can form the basis for resolving issues related to IE. Wiener combined the "received policy cluster" with his account of human nature, his "great principles of justice," and his critical skills in clarifying vague or ambiguous language. This way he was able to establish an efficient technique for evaluating the following IE issues:

- Address an ethical question or case pertaining to the infusion of IT into the society. Generally speaking, this would focus on the opportunities arising from technologies that have an impact on life, contentment, happiness, health, liberty, knowledge, prospects, and human principles.
- Provide explanations for any ambiguous or unclear notions and

philosophies that may be pertinent to a case or any issue.

- Check the possibility for applying laws, rules, customs, and principles that already exist in the society and uphold moral values and guide humans to tread on the ethical path.
- If customs, practices, and policies are not providing the required guidance to deal with an issue or resolve a situation, the great principles of justice should be used to find a fitting solution that will conform to the moral traditions of the civilization.

If the traditions, precedents, and policies that one starts with are embedded within a reasonably just society, then this method of analyzing and resolving IE issues will likely provide just solutions that can be assimilated into that society.

In the late 1940s and early 1950s, Wiener expressed unambiguously that, introducing the newly invented computing and IT, would usher in a new era in the society. This new "automatic age" will be the second industrial revolution. Continuous, relentless, and multidimensional efforts would be required, and this would bring about a change in every aspect of life.

According to Weiner, IT has dramatically altered human life and positioned them "in the presence of another social potentiality of unheard-of importance for good and for evil." (Wiener, 1954) Wiener predicted decades ago that an "information age" will emerge. He also predicted that the metaphysical and scientific basis that he envisaged can act as a guiding force for resolving and interpreting the ethical issues that information technologies may stimulate.

1.4.3. A Cybernetic View of Human Nature

Wiener's emphasized on the physical anatomy of humans and also the immense potential that they hold for developing themselves and innovate new processes. Wiener often compared humans to lesser evolved organisms to explain his view that humans are capable of remarkable achievements.

Cybernetics takes the view that the configuration of the machine or of the organism is an indicator of the competence in the execution of tasks that can be expected from it. The fact that the mechanical rigidity of the insect is such as to limit its intelligence while the mechanical fluidity of the human being provides for his almost indefinite intellectual expansion is highly relevant to the point of view of this book. Humans have a physiological advantage and intellectual capability over the rest of nature and can adapt themselves to the fundamental alterations in his living conditions. The human race can continue to be dominant only if they make use of their inherent, adaptive, learning faculties that they derive from their physiological structure (Wiener, 1954, pp. 57–58, italics in the original)

The physiology of humans empowers them to absorb a wide range of information from their environment, take in information about conditions and events within themselves. Human anatomy not just enables access to all the information but allows to reason, analyze, reflect, determine, and engage intellectually with the information obtained. Weiner inferred from all his research that the objective of human life was to thrive as an information-processing organism since they have the inherent ability to do so.

It is evident that humans possess the ability to absorb massive amounts of information, gather knowledge on an ongoing basis. Almost half of human life could be dedicated to learning and studies, since they are physically capable to do so unlike insects like ants. The two intrinsic characteristics of human sensorium are variety and possibility. This is because these two characteristics are a part of the structure of the human organism (Wiener, 1954, pp. 51–52).

1.5. DEVELOPMENT OF COMPUTER ETHICS

In the 50s and 60s, Nobert Wiener contributed profoundly to the field of IE, and this was wider than the more specific field of computer ethics. Wiener's principles and notions about IE id not restricted to computer ethics alone but can also be extended to other fields like Agent ethics, Internet ethics, and the ethics of nanotechnology, the ethics of bioengineering, even journalism ethics, and library ethics.

In the 1960s and early 1970s, even before Walter Maner came up with the term "computer ethics" and offered a definition in the field, progress was made in the exact field of computer ethics. For example, Donn Parker, who was a computer scientist at SRI International, had started to take notice of the illegal doings of computer professionals and began to study them. This was during the mid-1960s. The article "Rules of Ethics in Information Processing," was published by Parker in Communications of the ACM. This contained information about cases of computer crimes.

Parker also supervised the conception of the original Code of Professional Conduct for the Association for Computing Machinery (ACM). In 1973, the ACM adopted this code in due course. He also went on to release a number of publications on cybercrime. (Parker, 1979; Parker et al., 1990). In the latter half of the 1960s, a computer scientist at MIT named Joseph Weizenbaum created ELLIZA. This was a basic computer program that he called ELIZA. His intention was to offer a rough imitation of "a Rogerian psychotherapist engaged in an initial interview with a patient."

The reaction of people to his modest program, startled and dismayed Weizenbaum. For example, some computer scientists at MIT, who even though, were aware of how the ELIZA program worked, became emotionally involved with it. They even shared their personal views and opinions with them. Some psychiatrists deliberated that, ELIZA is proof that computers soon would perform automated psychotherapy.

The reactions to his invention made, Weizenbaum anxious that an "information-processing model" of human beings was reinforcing an already growing tendency among scientists, and even the public, to see humans as "mere machines." Consequently, he wrote the book Computer Power and Human Reason in 1976 in which he expressed his anxiety. Many scholars were influenced by this book and some speeches he gave in the various parts of the country. They began to contemplate about the impact that computing would have on society and morals.

1.5.1. Walter Maner and His Views on Computer Ethics

Walter Maner who was associated with Old Dominion University in Virginia coined the term "computer ethics" to refer that field of inquiry dealing with ethical problems aggravated, transformed or created that can be attributed to computers. Maner even offered a course on this subject at his university.

In the latter part of the 70s and the mid–80s the courses offered by Maner in the university gained a lot of popularity. He also offered a large number of courses and workshops aimed at educating people about computer ethics in the philosophy and computer science conferences all over America. In the year 1978, he launched his Starter Kit in Computer Ethics independently. Through this kit, he intended to assist the university teachers to plan courses on computer ethics.

The Starter Kit also contained suggestions for university prospectus, a rational explanation for including this course in the curriculum of the university, a list of the purposes of the course, some handy instruction on the teaching approach to be adopted, some topics that could be included like cyber-crime, privacy, and confidentiality, professional code of ethics.

The course offered by Maner in combination with the Starter Kit and the conferences he conducted influenced the students of America in the field of computer ethics. Several scholars began to concentrate on this new filed, and there was also an increase in the number of university courses that were offered on this subject.

Maner also generated a Starter Kit on Teaching Computer Ethics, basing it on his teaching experiences and research in the planned new field. He circulated copies of the kit to the attendees of the workshop he ran and speeches that he gave at philosophy conferences and computing conferences in America. The starter kit was published as a monograph in 1980, by the Helvetia Press and the National Information and Resource Center on Teaching Philosophy, headed by the present author.

1.6. PROFESSIONAL AND COMPUTER ETHICS

Donald Gotterbarn, in the early 1990s, supported a different emphasis within computer ethics. He was of the view that computer ethics should be perceived as professional ethics. It should be dedicated to the progress and improvement of standards of good practice and codes of conduct for computing professionals. In 1991 Gotterbarn published an article "Computer Ethics: Responsibility Regained," in which he quoted:

"There is little attention paid to the domain of professional ethics – the values that guide the day-to-day activities of computing professionals in their role as professionals. By computing professional, I mean anyone involved in the design and development of computer artifacts. The ethical decisions made during the development of these artifacts have a direct relationship to many of the issues discussed under the broader concept of computer ethics."

Gotternbarn wanted to contribute to the field of professional ethics, hence collaborated with other supporters of professional ethics like Simon Rogerson, Keith Miller, Dianne Martin and Chuck Huff in a large number of projects to enforce professional ethics in computer practitioners. Gotternbarn was already a part of ACM to generate the next version of its "Code of Ethics and Professional Conduct." This was adopted by ACM in 1992.

Gotterbarn along with his co-workers in ACM and the computer society of Institute of Electrical and Electronic Engineers (IEEE), established licensing standards for software engineers. He also spearheaded a joint task force of these two institutes to develop the "Software Engineering

Code of Ethics and Professional Practice" which were adopted by them in 1999. Gotterbarn also created the Software Engineering Ethics Research Institute (SEERI) at East Tennessee State University in the late 1990s. In the early 2000s, he co-created a computer software with Simon Rogerson called Software Development Impact Statements (SoDIS). The purpose was to support individuals and organizations to devise ethical "stakeholder analyses." The analysis would help in ascertaining the moral impact of software development projects.

The efforts of Gotterbarn and many other projects emphasized on professional responsibility and facilitated the professionalization and ethical maturation of computing practitioners.

In 1995, Krystyna Górniak-Kocikowska in her ETHICOMP95 presentation "The Computer Revolution and the Problem of Global Ethics," made a staggering prophecy. She predicted that computer ethics will gradually penetrate into all cultures worldwide and will emerge as global ethics. According to this "Gorniak hypothesis," regional ethical theories like Europe's Benthamite and Kantian systems, as well as the diverse ethical systems embedded in other cultures of the world, all derive from "local" histories and customs and are unlikely to be applicable worldwide. Gorniak opined that computer and IE have the possibility to deliver a global ethic that can cater to the new Information Age.

The computer revolution is expected to give birth to a new ethical theory that will emerge from computer ethics. This evolving field is expected to be even more significant than even its creators and supporters believed.

The nature of the Computer Revolution is unique. This suggests that ethics that emerge in the future will be universally accepted. It will be multidimensional in nature and truly global. It can also be considered global since it considers human actions and relations in its totality.

Computer networks are not affected by borders, and hence it can be said that computers have a universal presence. Computer ethics to a large extent can mean evolving global ethics.

It is crucial that regulations with respect to computers are drafted effectively. However, if these rules are not well accepted widely by most of the computer users, its implementation will be unsuccessful. Computer ethics will gain global character when it evolves into a global ethic.

The "Gorniak hypothesis" intended to cause a strong response, and it made a noteworthy contribution to the "uniqueness debate." Maner had asserted in ETHICOMP95 conference in his keynote address that IT "forces us to discover new moral values, formulate new moral principles, develop new policies, and find new ways to think about the issues presented to us."

Gorniak's hypothesis reiterated the same. However, Gorniak did not foresee that IE would pave the way for concepts that would be applicable globally. She projected that a global ethics theory would develop with time because the internet is universal and consequently the ethics conversation centering around it also has a global character.

Gorniak was accurate in her to prophesy. Global network, especially the internet, has been fundamental in connecting human beings worldwide. Computer ethics appears to be progressing into an expansive and even more significant field today. It might be rightly termed as "global IE." For the first time in history, steps are being taken on a global level, to formulate mutually agreed standards of conduct. Also, the need for securing human values and advancing them is being felt worldwide.

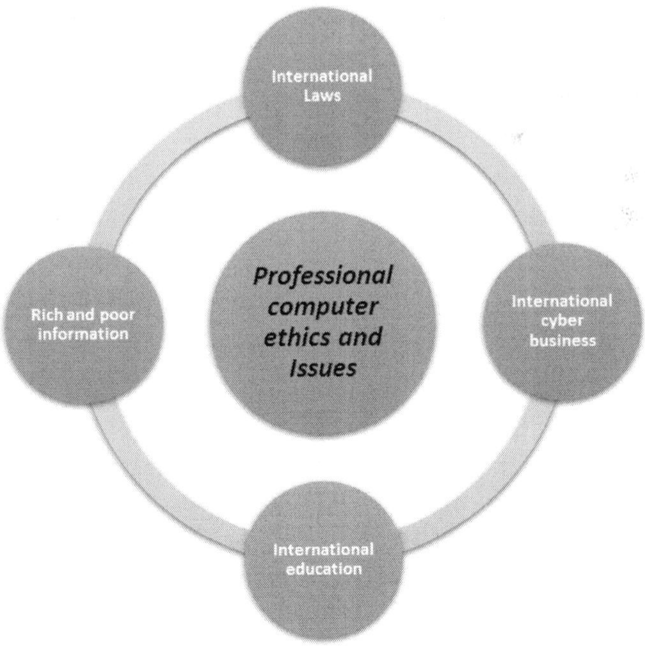

Figure 1.2: Computer Ethics in the professional world and issues related to it.

As a first, ethics, and values were discussed and transformed into a global context and were not restricted to a specific country or a region, unrestrained by the boundaries of culture and religion. This development can be considered as one of the most important social development in thc history of mankind). Some of the related global issues are discussed below (Figure 1.2):

1.6.1. International Laws

Over two hundred or more countries worldwide are interconnected by the internet. A significant question arises as to what laws would apply. For example, if an internet user in London wishes to protect their privacy, which law would protect his rights?

The local law of the UK would not apply to the rest of the world. There are a number of issues that require regulation over the internet like control of pornography, freedom of speech, protection of intellectual property, invasion of privacy. The task is even more daunting since so many countries are involved. When people of the two countries are involved in dealing over the internet, and one country finds the activity illegal, a question arises as to how the other country would deal with the matter.

1.6.2. International Cyber-Business

The globalization has driven the "cyberbusiness" worldwide, and it has grown exponentially. Countries with good infrastructure facilities have been able to leverage them to enjoy economic benefits. The countries that are not well equipped have not been able to do so. Some important issues that arise are:

- What will the outcome of the unequal expansion of "cyberbusiness" be?
- Will the laws and regulation of one country be binding on another?
- Will the disparity in income widen as a few countries become wealthier?
- Will all this result in political confrontations and war?

1.6.3. International Education

Information should be made available to everyone at an affordable price, be it downtrodden people in the developing nations or the rich. If this happens, for the first time ever, all humans on earth will be able to update themselves with the current affairs from a free press, will have access to artworks and documents from good libraries and museums all over the globe, will be able to understand traditions, customs, and political scenarios of all places on Earth.

The access to this "global education" has been unexpected and intense. The effect of this on political dictatorships, isolated communities, coherent cultures, religious practices, etc. has to be weighed. For example, if more recognized universities of the world start offering distance education programs over the internet, will that have an adverse impact on universities that are not that well recognized.

1.6.4. Rich and Poor Information

The disparity between developing and developed nation is widening. Even in the advanced countries, the gap between the poor and rich is alarming. A concern that arises is, when educational opportunities, business, and job prospects, services in the field of medicine, and other utilities on which humans depend, have to be accessed via the internet, the gap between the wealthy and the needy may further widen making matters worse.

1.7. FACTORS INFLUENCING INFORMATION ETHICS

There are many factors that impact and mold IE. There are some factors that have a humongous impact, and they are discussed below:

- **Globalization:** Globalization is undoubtedly the most significant development of this century. In this new era of globalization, there is widespread use of ICTs and openness in exchanging information. This has also given rise to conflicts among individuals and societies trying to proclaim supremacy over others.
- **More emphasis on individualism:** In today's world, people often prioritize personal well-being over social good as they tend to be more self-centered. Consequently, the demand for customized and personalized services has increased.
- **Privacy and information security:** The whole world is now a big network. Hence an apprehension that arises is privacy and security of all the data held in public and private databases. Information repositories like websites have to be secured properly. There is a growing concern among people about the confidentiality of the personal information held in these databases. It is the responsibility of the providers and handlers of this information to

keep them discrete and prevent them from falling into the wrong hands.

- **Diversification of 'information works':** The information professionals have a bigger responsibility than their forerunners. They have to play multiple roles apart from being just providers of information. They also become consultants, guides, coaches, technical specialists, translators, and others. They have to constantly upgrade their skills and competencies and acquire new ones to discharge their new responsibilities.
- **The conflict between 'right to information' and 'ethical use of information':** Countries all over the globe have passed laws to safeguard people's rights to obtain and utilize information. For instance, India passed the 'Right to Information Act' in 2005, and Bangladesh passed it in 2009. Nevertheless, security concerns and other such reasons, restrict access to classified information by the general public. An information professional often faces dilemmas when it comes to choosing between 'rights to information' and 'restricted use of information.'
- **Access to information:** Many libraries will also have to deal with the issue of universal access to information. According to Fernandez-Molina various public and professional declarations refer unequivocally to free and public access to information. For instance, individuals have the right to free and public access to information as per the British Library Association code of conduct.

It needs to be considered that, that if too much importance is given on providing service without charging for the same, it could result in a cash crunch for the information center and jeopardize its survival. It should be borne in mind that when a service is provided at no cost, its value is often depreciated. As a result, the respect and viability of the profession will be undermined.

- **Intellectual property rights:** Reproduction of information material through means like photocopying, faxing, scanning, and other such methods have become very easy with the invention of new technologies. Reproduction is now a hassle-free process, and this affects the rights of the holders of intellectual property detrimentally. It will now result in conflict between the information professional and owners of the information, with the former longing to obtain it a low price and the latter wanting to protect his own interest.

Commoditization of information has happened due to information now being categorized as raw materials. Information is now traveling across various sectors and carries a price tag. This is making it hard for less affluent people to procure and utilize information.

According to Schiller "In the reallocation of information resources now occurring throughout the economy from one set of users (the general population) to another (mostly corporate business users), one principle prevails. It is the market criterion – the ability to pay. This determines who will receive and who will be excluded from the benefits of the information lubricated economy."

Evidently, information professionals now face new moral dilemmas in determining their roles and responsibility in this complex 'infosphere' it is equally difficult to assess their own capability to support the less privileged population to protect their right to free information and use it productively.

1.8. THE EXPONENTIAL GROWTH OF INFORMATION AND COMPUTER ETHICS

The conceptualization of a new academic field and its advancement is dependent on collaboration among scholars and supporting services from universities, research centers in the form of courses, conferences, and academic journals. The year 1958 was critical for information and computer ethics, in this respect. The Strong foundation of the field was laid down by Johnson when he published his book Computer Ethics and a special issue of the journal Metaphilosophy in 1985. Moor's wrote the article "What is Computer Ethics?" which was also a brilliant curriculum material for this field.

Maner had put in humungous efforts and had also influenced other people to contribute to this field. Consequently, a generation of passionate computer science and philosophy scholars was born. This paved the way for exponential growth. It has to be noted that Maner was way ahead of his time when he laid down the foundation for computer and IE in the 1940s and 50s. It was only much later in the 80s when scholars and social thinkers followed his lead and developed this new field of computer and IE. The mid-1980s witnessed rapid advancement in the field of information and computer ethics, in the United States. The Research Center on Computing & Society was founded in 1987 in the Southern Connecticut State University. Soon after this the Director collaborated with Walter Maner and organized "the National Conference on Computing and Values (NCCV). This was funded by America's National Science Foundation. The aim was to foster cooperation among various professionals like computer scientists, philosophers, public leaders, law-makers, entrepreneurs, sociologists, psychologists, journalists, and others.

Another objective was to analyze and make progress in some of the important sub-fields of information and computer ethics. These areas included computer privacy, ownership of intellectual property, educating about computer ethics and helping persons with disabilities. The NCCV which was held in August 1991 witnessed the participation of various disciples along with the efforts of Bynum and Maner.

The NCCV was attended by over four hundred people from all states in America and other countries as well. The conference produced monographs, video programs, and an extensive bibliography and other computer ethics materials. This was distributed amongst several colleges and universities in the following years.

Various professional ethics advocates came forward which included among others Donald Gotterbarn, Keith Miller and Dianne Martin. Professional organizations also became involved. These included organizations like Computer Professionals for Social Responsibility, the Electronic Frontier Foundation, and the Special Interest Group on Computing and Society (SIGCAS) of the ACM. They led projects that centered on developing the professional responsibility of computer practitioners.

Information and computer ethics turned into an integral module of undergraduate computer science programs that Computer Sciences Accreditation Board accredited. In 1991 I "Computers, Freedom, and Privacy" conferences started to be organized annually. In 1992, the ACM also adopted an upgraded version Code of Ethics and Professional Conduct.

In 1995, Europe was also engulfed by the swift advancement made in the field of information and computer ethics. Maner joined hands with Simon Rogerson – a lecturer in De Montfort University in England. They jointly developed the Centre for Computing and Social Responsibility and organized the first computer ethics conference in Europe which was called ETHICOMP95. This conference was a huge success and attracted attendees from various countries in Europe. This conference was hugely responsible for giving birth to computer ethics scholars in Europe. The ETHCOMP traveled to many countries in Europe post-1995. It was held every 18 months and even moved to countries beyond Europe. Some of the countries to host this event were Poland, Greece, France, Spain, Portugal, China, and Japan. Encouraged by this far-reaching response, the Australian scholars John Weckert and Christopher Simpson with the backing of Bynum and Rogerson, established the Australian Institute of Computer Ethics in 1999. They also organized AICEC99 in Melbourne which was the first international computer ethics conference in that part of the globe. This has been followed by numerous AICE conferences.

Simon Rogerson was a prominent person in Europe in the rapid growth of information and computer ethics. His achievements include setting up the Centre for Computing and Social Responsibility at De Montfort University and co-heading the influential ETHICOMP conferences.

His contribution was also:

- He contributed towards adding computer ethics to De Montfort University's curriculum;
- He also created a graduate program with advanced computer ethics degrees which comprised PhDs; and
- Was responsible for co-founding and co-editing two computer ethics journals with Ben Fairweather. Those two journals were: The Journal of Information, Communication, and Ethics in Society in 2003 and the electronic journal The ETHICOMP Journal in 2004.

Rogerson was also part of the IT Committee of the British Parliament. He went on to participate in various computer ethics projects alongside agencies based in the European Union.

During the late 1990s and early 2000s, various computer ethics were developed in Europe. Some of the prominent examples of those developments are:

- In the 1990s, Luciano Floridi founded the IE Research Group at Oxford University.
- In 1997, Jeroen van den Hoven created of the Computer Ethics: Philosophical Enquiry series of conferences (CEPE). This which was held alternately in America and Europe.
- In 1999 Van den Hoven's developed the journal Ethics and IT.
- In the same year, Rafael Capurro established the ICIE.

- In 2004 Rafael Capurro's developed International Review of IE a journal.
- In 2005, Bernd Carsten Stahl's created The International Journal of Technology and Human Interaction.

In conclusion, it can be said that computer ethics development has multiplied exponentially. New researches, new establishments, new newsletters, new research centers, study materials, websites, university programs, college degree courses, and illustrious professorships have contributed to this growth. As further advancement is made in information and computer ethics, additional subjects and topics continue to surface.

Various new topics have emerged in this field of ethics which include robot's ethics, cyborg ethics, "open source movement," electronic government, global IE, IT and genetics, computing for developing countries, computing, and terrorism, ethics, and nanotechnology. The above-mentioned sub-fields are only a few among the various disciplines that have developed.

The field of computer ethics is relatively new in comparison to other scholarly disciplines. It came into existence in the late 1940s when Norbert Weiner created it. The progress made was very slow since Wiener's perceptions, and intuitions were far ahead of his time. Since 1985 information and computer ethics has advanced exponentially. America was the torchbearer in this respect followed by Europe and then the rest of the world.

1.9. CONCLUSION

IE has made significant advancement over the years. Other disciplines have also embraced this field in the last few decades.

The United States was the pioneer in establishing this field. The works of various scholars and researchers have addressed several issues in their work including privacy policies, right to information, the fair use of information, and ethical dilemmas among others. However, there were no courses that were specifically dedicated to the ethical issues in this field. When such courses were first offered in U.S. IE broadened its horizon to embrace IT, computer ethics, and moral dilemmas in the management of information systems and information in society.

Unfortunately, even today most schools of library and information science do not offer courses specifically pertaining to ethical issues, and these issues are presented in the context of other issues. It can be summarized that IE is a complex and evolving field that has been influenced immensely by other disciplines, customs, and perspectives.

REFERENCES

1. Bynum, T., (2004). *Computer Ethics: Basic Concepts and Historical Overview*. [eBook] Available at: http://www.dcc.ufrj.br/~jonathan/compsoc/Computer+Ethics%20+Basic+Concepts+and+Historical+Overview.pdf [Accessed 31 Oct. 2018].
2. Carbo, T., (n.d.). *Understanding Information Ethics and Policy: Integrating Ethical Reflection and Critical Thinking into Policy Development*. [pdf] Available at: https://www.ideals.illinois.edu/bitstream/handle/2142/15106/PA8_iconf08.pdf [Accessed 31 Oct. 2018].
3. Floridi, L., (2006). *Information Ethics, its Nature and Scope*. [eBook] Available at: http://citeseerx.ist.psu.edu/viewdoc/download?doi=10.1.1.499.6848&rep=rep1&type=pdf [Accessed 31 Oct. 2018].
4. Floridi, L., (2010). *The Cambridge Handbook of Information and Computer Ethics* (pp. 3–20). Cambridge: Cambridge University Press.
5. Himma, K., & Tavani, H., (2008). *The Handbook of Information and Computer Ethics* (pp. 1–69). Hoboken, N.J.: Wiley.
6. *Introduction to Computer Ethics,* (n.d.). Chapter 1. [pdf] Available at: https://www.cs.uct.ac.za/mit_notes/ethics/pdfs/chp01.pdf [Accessed 31 Oct. 2018].
7. Plato.stanford.edu., (2015). *Computer and Information Ethics (Stanford Encyclopedia of Philosophy)*. [online] Available at: https://plato.stanford.edu/entries/ethics-computer/ [Accessed 31 Oct. 2018].
8. Rorty, M., (n.d.). *Introduction to Ethics*. [pdf] Available at: https://www.ache.org/pubs/filermanch1.pdf [Accessed 31 October 2018].
9. Ward Bynum, T., (2000). *A Very Short History of Computer Ethics (Text Only) – The Research Center on Computing & Society*. Available at: http://www.cs.utexas.edu/~ear/cs349/Bynum_Short_History.html [Accessed 31 Oct. 2018].
10. Brandt, D. and Henning, K. (2002). Information and Communication Technologies: Perspectives and their Impact on Society. AI & SOCIETY, [online] 16(3), pp.210-223. Available at: https://link.springer.com/article/10.1007/s001460200018 [Accessed 14 Mar. 2019].
11. WIENER, N. (1954). *CYBERNETICS IN HISTORY*. [ebook] Available at: http://neoscenes.net/teach/cu/2012_2/atls2000_mit/pdfs/Wiener-1954-Cybernetics_in_History.pdf [Accessed 14 Mar. 2019].

2

Information Technology and Moral Methodology

CONTENTS

Information technology (IT) is defined as an essential part of the practices and institutions of postindustrial society. Also, it is a source of hard moral questions, and hence it is a probing as well as a relevant field of moral theory. The chapter talks about IT and moral methodology of computer ethics, the challenges involved in IT. IT is a universal technology. This is not just regarding the computers, networks or other electronic devices. It is also regarding the information that everyone should be careful of what the IT has. The chapter further describes the future concerns of IT in the context of acceleration of change, artificial intelligence (AI), artificial life (ALife) and robotics.

2.1. INTRODUCTION

IT is being considered as omnipresent within the lives of the general public across the world. Such technologies have taken up various forms viz: smartphones, AI, and robotics, personal computers, internet technologies, etc. The list is constantly growing, and the modern forms of these kinds of technologies are working in every aspect of daily life.

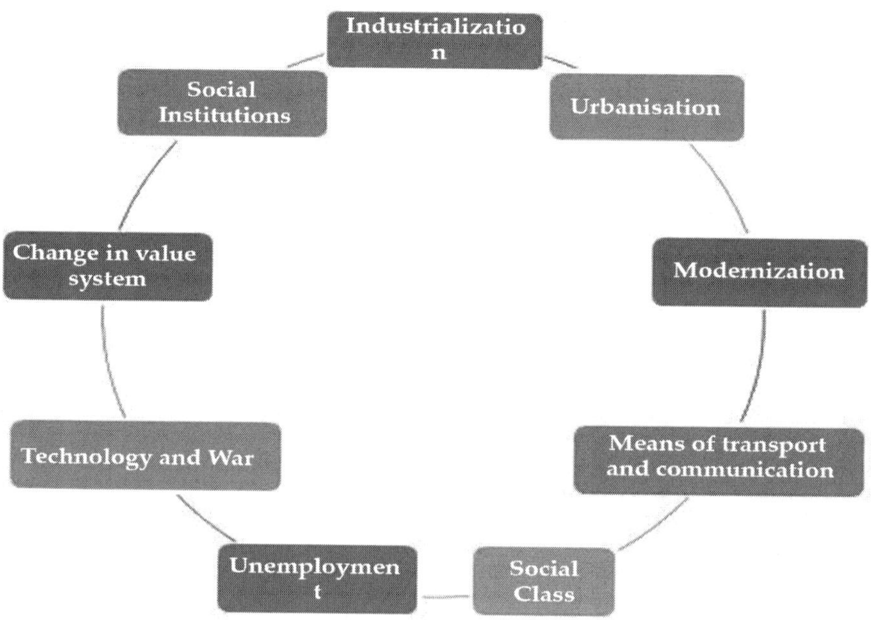

Figure 2.1: Impact of technology change on society.

Source: http://www.sociologyguide.com/social-change/impact-of-technology-change.php

With all new interfaces, new types of computations have evolved in the market and users with the help of advanced operating systems and various other applications are making it possible to cross the moral values of computer and information ethics (IE). In a few instances, these technologies are developing advanced ways of human interaction with each other. But, human interaction through different technical sources is only productive if it does not cross the ethical lines (Figure 2.1).

IT is being utilized for the purpose of recording, organizing the pertaining information, communicating, as well as synthesizing them with the help of the utilization of the computer technologies. The information, in its own terms, can be implied as any data that is being useful, the existing instructions, or the content containing meaningful texts or messages.

Sadly, no such entirely satisfying as well as philosophically robust description or definition is gettable, although there pertains a minimum of two great points to give it a start.

Shannon working in the forties at Bell Labs produced a mathematical theory of communication (1948). In this work, various experiences have been used in telephone technologies and cryptography to work out a formulation based upon mathematics defining how syntactical information can be further turned into such a signal that is transferred to alleviate noise or different extraneous signals that can be decoded by the receiver of the message.

The affirmation is that the person available would not be able to have a sound understanding related to the inputs and thus, would not be able to interpret what all the system is saying being its output, and it is then being considered as baseless manipulation of the symbol in accordance with them.

IT has a great impression on the philosophical study of information as well as logic. In this context, the field logic is utilized as a method to analyze the information along with the use of information as a method to build the base of logic itself.

All the issues that have been discussed seem to be appealing, but they are, in general, segregate arguments that might not certainly be getting sorted or resolved, prior to the entrance of people in a discussion based on the IT as well as the moral values.

2.2. THE MORAL CHALLENGES OF INFORMATION TECHNOLOGY

The transfer from one set of dominant information technologies to the other is ethically combative. Socrates survived in the phase of long transition from an oral tradition to an advanced IT comprising writing down words as well as information and eventually, collecting those writings into scrolls and books.

Well- acclaimed Socrates was somewhat unsympathetic to writing, and all the scholars used to have a claim that they have never written anything which would anyhow down them. On a contrast, almost everyone was just aware regarding the argument of Socrates in opposition to the writing part, as his student used to neglect his teacher and later, wrote them down in the form of a dialogue, which was known as "Phaedrus."

To the end of this dialogue, Socrates with his friend Phaedrus discusses that the "...conditions which make it (writing) proper or improper." Socrates says a tale of an Egyptian God that has been named Theuth who provides the gift of writing to a king known as Thamus.

2.2.1. The Fundamental Character of Information Technologies

In the initial stage of the revolution of IT, Richard Mason had provided with the suggestion regarding the upcoming transformations or the changes within the information technologies, for instance: their respective parts or the roles in the effects of education as well as economy that would be necessitated the process of rethinking about the social contract.

Various researchers got really worried that they would further challenge the privacy, accuracy, property, and accessibility (PAPA) and to secure their society, they "... should frame a new social contract, one that assures everyone the right to complete their own human potential" (Mason, 1986, p. 11).

The legit theorist Larry Lessig provided them with the warning that the rate at which the changes are taking place in IT is so fast that it would be leaving the steady as well as the contemplative procedures of policies, related to the law and politics, behind, and thus, being an outcome of all these, such technologies would certainly become extralegal or lawless.

This is because of the fact that when a law is written to restrain, few forms of the copyright infringement enabled by a specific file-sharing technology, that technology has become outdated and users are on to something else that enables even more copyright infringement (Lessig, 1999). Information technologies store, communicate, organize, and synthesize the information. For instance, a book is a kind of information record, a telephone is utilized to communicate information, and the Dewey decimal system categorizes the information.

Ultimately, the major focus would not be just on how the IT possess an impact on the moral institutions but also how it would be leading to certain changes or transformations within the respective nature of the moral reasoning.

Many things have been discussed about the information, being the technology of morality as well as how the researchers would be programming those applications along with the robots to have an interaction with them, in a manner, which would be morally acceptable.

2.2.2. Moral Values in Information Recording

Power is the control of information, and in the economy of information, it might be the eventual form of political power. Today, we are living in a world which is full of data and the technology to produce, record, store a huge amount of data has rapidly developed.

Here the primary and moral concern is that when the data is collected, stored, and eventually accessed, it is dynamic that this be done in a way that reason can be observed as fair and also in the best interests of every party involved.

Varied social institutions which conventionally used to practice these powers are the things viz: the pertaining religious organizations, various institutions, officials within the healthcare sector, libraries, several agencies of the government, banks as well as the corporations.

These kinds of entities have easy access to the information that is stored that further provides them a fixed amount of power over their constituencies and customers. These days every citizen has access to the stored information without the requirement of using the conventional mediators of that information and hence a huge individual share of the social power.

The last and the final concern or the cause of worry is that the information technologies, which are currently storing their respective data of the user in the 'cloud,' that means the data which has been stored on the device secretively placed from the user and thus, are not being possessed or functioned by those users only, but then the data is accessible from anywhere, where the user belongs, and on any of the provided device they seem to be utilizing. As the personal information and data is very important to secure, the third parties that provide cloud services require to recognize the accountability of the trust the user is placing in them. If a person uploads all of his or her photographs to a service such as Flickr and somehow, they were to delete or lose them, this would be a kind of disastrous mistake that might be possible to repair.

2.2.3. Moral Values in Communicating and Accessing Information

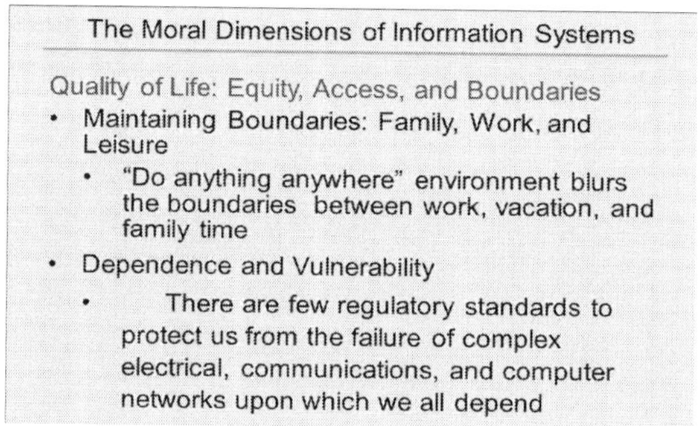

Figure 2.2: The moral dimensions of information systems.

Source: https://slideplayer.com/slide/4499359/

The primary and moral values that appear to be under stress from these changes are confidentiality, privacy, trust, ownership, and veracity of the information being transferred in these advanced ways. Who has an ultimate say whether or not a few information regarding a user is communicated or not? Who is permitted to sell medical records, email, financial records, browsing history, etc.? If there is no control over this process, then how moral rights can be enforced on privacy? For example, Alan Westin has argued in the very initial stages of the advanced digital information technologies regarding the hold of the right to the personal information of someone, which was being considered as the core for having maintenance of the secrecy or privacy. If further follows that if privacy is being cared, then people must give access control to the personal data and information to the individual. Various corporate entities fight this idea for the reason that data and information regarding users have primarily become a commodity in the digital world improving the great fortunes of corporations such as

Facebook or Google. Certainly, there is a major deal of utility, and every person attains from the services offered by internet search companies like Google and social networks as Facebook.

It may also be opined that it is, in real, just an exchange of fair that people are receiving as they are presenting with the outcome of searches as well as the various other application in exchange of nothing and they are offsetting the cost, which has been associated with the creation of those respective worthy services, by the process of gathering the required data from various individual users who all can be monetized in the several pertaining profitable ways.

A key component of the profit model for these corporations is based on focused advertising where the information gathered on the user is utilized to aid analyze advertising that will be very efficient on specific user based on her or his search history and various other online behaviors.

To this end, they recommend that we assume in the context of limited access to information instead of strict personal control of the information. Security of information is another effective moral value that influences the access and information of user information.

In case, the hold of the information has been granted to the respective third parties in the form of exchange for the services that has been provided by them, then, such entities should also be considered responsible for the limitation or the restriction on the possession of the right to that information by the other people who may want to utilize it for the wrong purposes.

With the enough information, the complete identity of a person can be stolen and further utilized to facilitate larceny and fraud. This kind of crime has rapidly grown since the beginning of digital information technologies. The victims of these kinds of crimes can have their lives ruined as they attempt to reconstruct such things as their credit rating as well as bank accounts.

The complexity or the hardship in acquiring the entire security of the digital platform has been placed on the fact that the moral value relating to the security might get trapped in conflict with the moral values belonging to the sharing and the openness, and within them, the rest of the values that have provided with the guidance to many of the inceptive builders of IT.

Provided that the information technologies are capable of making such unethical behaviors much probable, then it can be opposed regarding the structure of cyberspace itself implicitly tends to do the endorsement of such unethical behavior. Since the capabilities of the design of IT impacts the lives of their users, the moral commitments of the designers of such kind of technologies may eventually command the course society will take, and the commitments to moral values will be determined then by various technologists.

Presuming we are justified in conceding access to few stores of the information that we might be in control of, there is a responsibility to assure that the information is accurate, useful as well as truthful. A simple experiment will definitely show those information technologies may have few issues in this context.

Loading up of numerous distinct search engines and then typing the identical search terminologies in all of them, each of search engine would be provided with the distinct outcomes, and many of those searches will certainly deviate greatly from one another.

This further depicts that every service utilizes a distinct proprietary algorithm for representing the user with outcomes from their search. It then follows that not every search is equal and the accuracy, truthfulness, and utility of the outcomes will depend majorly on which search provider you are utilizing and how much user information is shared with this provider.

All the given searches have been filtered by several algorithms so that they could be able to make an assurance that all the information that is believed by the provider of search, as important or essential to the user themselves is being listed first. As the pertaining algorithms have not been made public and thus, are considered to be tightly held secrets of the trade, the users have been investing their trust in such processes of filtration.

Again, the ease and secrecy of utilization that IT offers can enable fraudulent practices like clickjacking. Pettit in 2009 recommends that this must cause us to reexamine the role that moral values like reliance and trust play in a world full of information technologies.

Whilst most of this gap has been operated by the various economics, Charles Ess observed that there pertains an issue with the forces pertinent to the novel forms of the cyber have enabled ethnocentrism as well as colonialism, which can restrain the need or wants of all those people who are outside the West to have a participation within this novel "Global Metropolis."

John Weckert notes that the cultural distinction in giving and taking fault to play a major role in the design of more democratic information technologies. Others also argue that fundamental moral concerns such as privacy are differently weighed in Asian cultures.

2.2.4. Moral Values in Organizing and Synthesizing Information

Additionally, to the storing and communicating the data and information, various information technologies systematize the organization of information and mechanically authoring or synthesizing or acting on modern information. Norbert Wiener first established a theory of automated information synthesis which he then called *Cybernetics* (Wiener, 1954)).

Wiener comprehended that a machine could be planned to collect the information regarding the world, descend logical inferences regarding that information which would indicate positive actions, which the machine could ultimately implement, all without any direct input from a human agent.

Wiener rapidly saw that if his cybernetics vision was apprehended, there would be incredible moral concerns elevated by such machines and he sketched some of them in his book, *The Human Use of Human Beings*.

Weiner have argued that, whilst such types or forms of technology might have had great impacts on the moral, it was still viable to be enterprising as well as providing with the guidance regarding technology in varied manner that would be helping in having an increment within the abilities of the moral reasoning, belonging to both the machines as well as the human beings.

Here is a condition where a part of IT was making decisions regarding the prospect of immoral activity taking place that gives rise to a small amount of damage to the person that it was trying to aid. Gradually, machines make significant life-changing financial decisions related to people without many mistakes from human agents.

Whether or not, a person will be provided with a credit card, the price that he has to pay for insurance, mortgage loan, etc., is usually determined by a machine. For example, if a person applies for a credit card, the machine will then look for few data points such as credit record, salary, the economic condition of the area, etc. and then evaluate the probability that a person will default on the credit card.

Such possibility will either pass the plethora of embracement or not and thus, helps in determining if one is being provided with the card or not. The machine holds the potential of learning to make great judgments, provided with the outcomes regarding the prior decisions it has already made.

This type of machine learning, as well as forecasting, is based upon the intricate logic and mathematics, this intricacy may consequence in somewhat humorous instances of mistaken predictions as defined in the anecdote above, or it might be more exciting.

For instance, the program may understand the data about the identity of one's friends and connections, his or her fresh purchases, and other gladly accessible social data, which might consequence in the incorrect classification of that person as a latent terrorist, hence changing that person's life in a strongly negative way.

All these are entirely dependent on the structure or the design of the learning as well as the algorithm of forecasting, things which have conventionally been held as a secret, so that it is actually very difficult to provide with the justification of the preciseness of the forecasting.

2.3. THE MORAL PARADOX OF INFORMATION TECHNOLOGIES

Various issues raised are the consequence of the moral paradox of IT. Various users' desires information to be rapidly available and reliant to utilize and desire that it must come at very cost.

These users desire sensitive and important to be stable, secure, and reliable. Increasing the value of rapid and low cost decreases the capability of providing high-quality and secured information. The reverse of it is also true. Hence, the developers of information technologies are continually faced with making rough compromises.

The inceptive pioneer of web Stewart Brand have summed up greatly in his well- acclaimed quote, which states that on the one hand, the provided information requires to be costly, but it is actually so valuable.

The right information at the right time at the right place just transforms life. Whereas, information must be free as the cost of acquiring it is lower all the time. As these opposing moral values are really not possible to resolve, they are probably to continue to be at the center of the moral debate in the application and framing of information technologies in the coming days.

2.4. SPECIFIC MORAL CHALLENGES AT THE CULTURAL LEVEL

At the end of the 20th century, the term web 2.0 started to surface, and it basically referred to the advanced method that the global web was being utilized as a way for sharing of information, collaboration, and a change in the approach of web designers to comprise user-centered experiences on the websites.

Whilst, the real structure of the world wide web, in the year 1989 by the creator of it, has always been the one which has been included in accordance with the norms or the context of meeting other people and thus, cooperating with them online, wherein the users ultimately agreed to entirely utilize such potential by the year 2004, at the time when the first web 2.0 conference got held by O'Reilly Media.

The new kind of "augmented reality" is usually enabled by the fact that various people carry GPS facilitated smartphones and various other portable systems with them upon which they can easily run different applications that let them to interact with their neighbor and also with their computers at the same point of time, possibly looking at an item through a camera in their system. These technologies basically come up with their own conduct of issues and challenges.

2.4.1. Social Media and Networking

Social networking is defined as a term which is further given to different sites as well as applications that enables online social interactions focused upon information sharing with another user known as friends. Today, the most popular site is Facebook. Adding to it, there are Twitter, Instagram, Snapchat are also there.

There pertain numerous moral values which all these existing websites ask to be present within the question. Shannon Vallor, has provided with the reflection on how all the sites viz Facebook has transformed or even has challenged the respective standard of friendship. The basic analysis of such friendship was wholly based on the Aristotelian theory relating to the friendship (Figure 2.3).

Figure 2.3: Social media and networking sites.

Source: https://online-id.nl/introductie-voor-social-media/

Aristotle debated that humans realize a true and good life by virtuous friendships. Further, valor notes that there are four major dimensions of 'virtuous friendship' of Aristotle, namely empathy, reciprocity, shared life and self-knowledge, and that the three of them are available social media in different ways that sometimes can empower the friendship.

Johnny Hartz Soraker debates for an insignificant understanding of online friendship instead of a rush to the normative judgment on the assets of virtual friends. Issues related to privacy abound in the utilization of social media.

Following Mason, James Parrish recommends four key policies that a social media user must follow so as to assure ethical concern for the privacy of others:

While sharing the information on social networking sites, it is mandatory to consider the confidentiality of the personal information of a particular individual as well as the privacy of others' information who may connect to the information that is being shared.

While sharing information on social networking sites, it is the major concern of an individual who wants to share information, to validate the correctness of the information before sharing it with others.

A user of social networking site should never post any information related to themselves that in future they might want to retract. Additionally, the user should not post any information that is the product of the mind of any other individual, as once the information is shared on these sites, it will be very difficult to retract.

It is the major concern of every user of the social networking site to validate the authenticity of a person before permitting the person access to the information that is shared.

These systems are not framed to openly invade on the privacy of the individual. But as these services are free, there is a potential economic driver for the providers of services to yield at least some information regarding the activities of their users on the site so as to sell the information to different advertisers for direct marketing.

Such marketing can happen with the respective providers, only be selling the rights to the data of the users, which has been made incognito, so that the advertiser would probably be knowing regarding the places where the user prefers to buy a pair of jeans, but they are not being provided with the exact information or the identity, specifically, of that person.

2.4.2. Online Games and Worlds

The very first moral effect one comes across when anticipating online games is the propensity for these games to represent sexism and violence. There are various news stories that claim a kind of cause and effect relationship between real violence and violence in computer games.

The assert that the violence happening within the video games possess a causal connection or link with the occurrence of the actual violence that has robustly being evaluated by the various social scientists. However, many of the other scientists have argued that as such connection or relationship is being considered as tenuous at their bests, and that the actual problem at hand is the impact of such games possess on the moral character of the respective person.

The connection they possess is that the people who tend to design might be realizing that they are making up with the space wherein the people are being intended to spend larger parts of their lives and thus, gets entangled in those actual social as well as economic activities and thus, the designers are required to have a hold of the moral responsibilities, which are almost equivalent to those who might be writing a constitution of politics.

As per Purcell, there is a very small obligation to egalitarianism or democracy by those who develop and owe online games, and it requires to be discussed if a greater number of people spend time living in the virtual societies.

2.4.3. The Lure of the Virtual in Game Worlds

A determined concern regarding the utilization of computers and mainly computer games is that this might result in anti-social isolation and behavior. With the arrival of huge multiplayer games and video games designed for the family purpose, the social isolation hypothesis is quite hard to believe (Figure 2.4).

Figure 2.4: The lure of the virtual in game worlds.

Source: http://www.bostonherald.com/entertainment/movies/2018/03/steven_spielberg_explores_lure_of_virtual_vs_real_worlds

However, these games increase the gender-related equality issues. James Ivory applied online reviews of these games to do a study that represents that male outnumbers females in games, and also those images that are in games tend to be excessively sexualized.

Marcus Johansson has provided with the suggestion that people might be capable of eliminating the virtual immortality through the punishments associated with the virtual crimes along with the virtual penalties so that they could be able to enhance or improve much ethical communities being virtual.

The media has increased moral concerns regarding the way that childhood has been changed by the application of IT. Now, various applications are designed especially for babies and toddlers with educational applications or sometimes just for entertainment purpose so as to help keep the children engaged while their parents are busy.

This has provided with the encouragement to the children to have an interaction with the pertaining computers from an age which is as early as possible. As much of the children might be gullible to the manipulation of media like in case of advertising, it is required for people to ask if such practices are morally acceptable or not.

Based on the specific application being used, it may motivate solitary play that may further lead to the isolation, but others are more involving with the parents as well as the children playing. It must be noted that pediatricians have recommended that there are no known advantages to early media application among young children.

2.4.4. The Technological Transparency Paradox

One may think why the services of social media tend to be of free of use, but none the less, usually make great benefits for the private organizations that provide these kinds of services. It is not a deep secret that the way these organizations make benefit is by selling of the information that the social networking sites users are uploading to the system.

More users imply to more information that has been provided by them, and the greater the worth that is inculcating that respective information becomes.

The social value of owning this is quite doubtful, but the economic value is undeniable. When this was written, Mark Zuckerberg has constantly been grouped in the top ten billionaires by the Forbes Magazine.

A success built on offering a free service to the world. What companies like Facebook do charge for our services, like focused advertising, which let third-party organizations to use information that users have offered to the social media applications?

The outcome is that advertisements bought on an application like Facebook are most probable to be seen as beneficial for workers who are likely to go for these products just by clicking. The personal and more detailed information shared, the more beneficial it will be to the organization that it is shared with.

The thorough explicitness of connecting greatly and sharing their personal information with the various companies has been encouraged. All the people who tend to make the utilization of those networking technologies, generally receives great worth, in terms of the evidence by the great growth of the pertaining technology.

Shannon Vallor, a philosopher, accounts the trend of transparency as a form of what she calls the "Technological Transparency Paradox". She further notes that those in favor of developing technologies to encourage radically transparent societies, do so under the principle that this directness will raise accountability as well as democratic ideals.

But the irony is that the craze of such explicitness usually tends to acquire just the exact opposite along with the organizations that are greatly accountable, and also, which have not been selected democratically, possessing the information which can be utilized to enfeeble the democratic societies.

Indeed, the user is radically transparent and open to the organization. The algorithms that are used to gather the data and the third parties that this information is shared with is not subjected to the accountability and is opaque. The users of these technologies are required to be very transparent, but the organizations profiting off the information are not needed to be equally transparent.

2.5. MALWARE, SPYWARE, AND INFORMATIONAL WARFARE

Computer virus and malware threats continue to increase at a surprising rate. Professionals in security industry report that though few kinds of malware attacks like spam are dropping out of the fashion, advanced kind of attacks like Ransomware, cryptocurrency, and the cloud computing infrastructure hacking are on the upsurge, surpassing any small relief observed in the slowing down of older forms of attack (Figure 2.5).

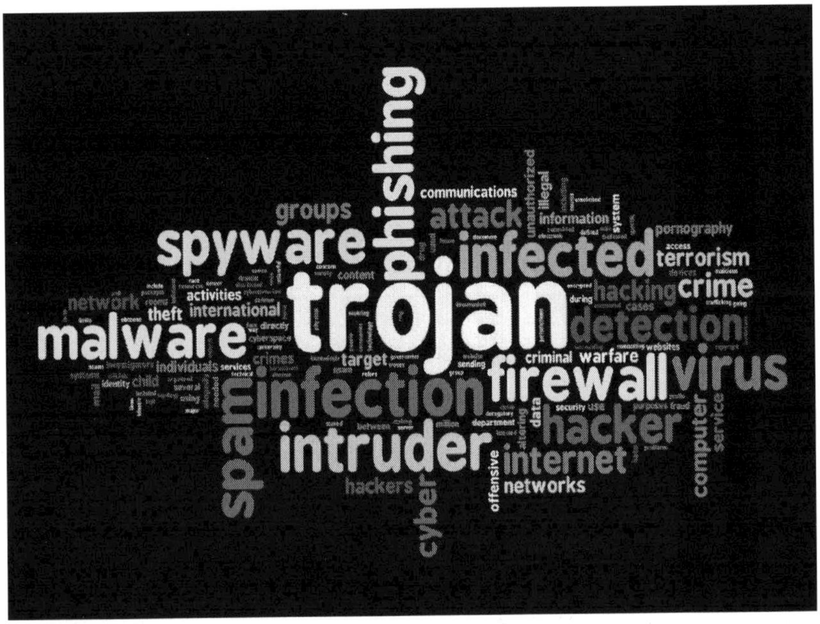

Figure 2.5: Malware, spyware, and informational warfare.

Source: http://globaltechconsultants.org/?q=content/what-difference-between-virus-worm-trojan-and-rootkit

These types of activities will be with us for sure in the near future. In context with the criminal activity of production of malware, related, and more ambiguous activities such as hacktivism, hacking, informational warfare, and commercial spyware must be considered.

All of the respective topics have a hold of their own poised moral ambivalence. It is now required to have an exploration of much of them. Whilst, there might persist great agreement regarding the cautious spreading up of the malware, which is considered to be having a questionable morality, there pertains an appealing question regarding the morality of the protection of malware as well as the software which is related to the antivirus.

With the increase in malicious software, there has been a constant increase in the security industry which is a kind of multibillion-dollar market. With all of the money spent on security software, there appears no decrease in the production of the virus.

The modus operandi of anti-virus relating to the receiving up of sample, having an analysis regarding the sample, adding on the detection for the required sample, performing assurance for the quality, making up of an update, and thus, ultimately sending those created updates to their respective users that in turn leaves a great window of opportunity for the antagonist, even after having an assumption regarding the users of the update of anti-virus, on a regular basis.

This gap is basically oppressed by malware producers, and in this model, there is any security hole that is not possible to fill. Hence, it is essential that security professionals do not exaggerate their capability of system protection, by the time an advanced malicious program is patched and discovered, it has done specific damage, and currently, there is no way to stop this.

This is not a completely new approach. Originally, it was recommended by the computer scientist, George Ledin in his *Communications of the ACM* editorial, "Not Teaching Viruses and Worms is Harmful" (2005). This notion does run counter to the popular opinion related to the ethics of learning as well as deploying malware.

Majority of these attacks appears to be probing for weaknesses, but they can confound the internet of countries like the cyber-attacks on Estonia in 2007 and those in Georgia which happened in the year 2008. While the Georgian and Estonian attacks were mainly designed to obscure communication in the target countries more recently informational warfare has been utilized to enable remote sabotage.

The popular Stuxnet virus earlier used to attack the nuclear centrifuges of Iran that is perhaps considered to be one of the great examples or instances of weaponized software that is actually capable of making secretively spoiling the physical facilities.

The primary challenge of informational warfare is defining how to utilized weaponized information technologies in such a way that honors the commitment of individuals to legal warfare. As warfare is a kind of questionable endeavor, it would be desirable if information technologies could be leveraged to reduce violent combat.

One might be possessing an argument of the great precise information that has been provided to all the decision makers at the time of war, which possess the requirement of providing with assistance so that they could make their decisions better, on the field of battle.

Whereas, these advance form of informational warfare abilities may permit states to involve in continual low-level conflict avoiding efforts for peacemaking that may need political compromise.

2.6. FUTURE CONCERNS

It has already been mentioned in the introduction that the information technologies are being in the consistent phase of the transformation as well as the advancement. The internet technologies which have been carrying great social changes that has been rarely imaginable a few years back prior to when they first appeared.

Even though a person may not be capable of foreseeing all probable future information technologies, and it is essential to try to assume the changes, a person probably observes in evolving technologies. James Moor contends that the moral philosophers require to pay specific attention to evolving technologies and aid influence the design of these kinds of technologies so as to motivate advantageous moral results. The following sections contain few of the potential technological concerns.

2.6.1. Acceleration of Change

An IT has a very interesting pattern of growth that has been seen since the establishment of industries. Gordon E. Moore, an Intel engineer found that the number of components that could be mounted on an IC, i.e., integrated circuit almost doubled every year for a slight economic cost, and further he thought it might last that way for next ten years or so from the time he found it in the year 1965.

This process is not restricted to the chips of computer only. Various forms of information technologies can be found in it. The latent power of the accelerating change has taken the thoughts of Ray Kurzweil, the futurist, and the inventor.

There has also been supporting for the thesis from the community of technology with institutes like the Acceleration Studies Foundation, the Singularity Institute, Future of Humanity Institute, and H+. The reaction of philosophers to this hypothesis has been really mixed but very crucial.

Similarly, Sullins (2006) contends that there is generally a quasi-religious facet to the transhumanism acceptance that is devoted to few results like uploading of consciousness of humans into the computer as a method to attain immortality, and that the receiving of transhumanist hypothesis impacts the values implanted in the computer technology, which can be hostile or dismissive to the body of human being.

Not every philosopher is critical of transhumanism, as an instance Nick Bostrom (2008) of the Future of Humanity Institute at Oxford University claims that putting the feasibility argument aside, we must accomplish that there are distinct posthumanism forms that would eventually lead to long as well as valuable lives and that it would be a very good thing for humans to become posthuman if and only if it is possible at all.

2.6.2. Artificial Intelligence and Artificial Life

AI is defined as various longstanding research projects which are aimed at constructing information technologies that display few or all contexts of problem-solving and human level intelligence.

AI as well as ALife are wide research projects that challenge the simple explanation. Here, the emphasis is on the moral values that these technologies influence and the way these technologies are programmed so as to affect morale and emotional concern.

- **Artificial Intelligence (AI):** Alan Turing is attributed with a significant research project that would come to be called an AI in his seminal 1950 paper "Computing Machinery and Intelligence (Figure 2.6)."

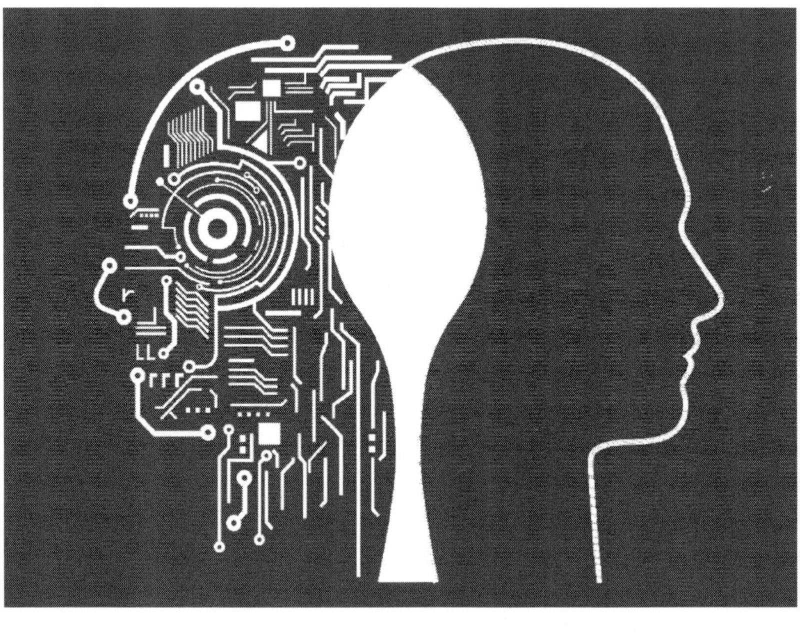

Figure 2.6: Artificial intelligence.

Source: https://uccexpress.ie/science-corner-artificial-intelligence-its-life-jim-but-not-as-we-know-it/

He further defined the "imitation game," where a computer tries to fool a human interlocutor that it is not a computer but another human. In the year 1950, he made the famous statement that "It has been supposed that in about fifty years' time.... one will be capable of speaking to machines thinking without expecting to be denied."

Luciano Floridi (2011a), for example, debated that as AI has been very effective as a source of expanding our own intelligence, but being a branch of cognitive science that is concerned with the intelligence production, AI has been a miserable disappointment.

The opposite opinion has been also contended, and some argue that the Turing Test has now been passed or at least that programmers are on the edge of doing so.

For example, it was stated by the BBC in 2014 that the Turing Test had been approved by a program that could influence the judges that it was a 13-year-old Ukrainian boy, but many experts remain skeptical.

Sullins (2006) counters this argument by remarking that consciousness is not needed for moral agency. For example, living, and non-living organisms and the non-human animals present in our environment should be conferred few moral rights and any AI able of Turing would have moral rights and duties both, irrespective of its status as a cognizant being (Sullins, 2006).

AI is able to create machines that can effectively converse in simple ways with humans as proved by Apple Siri, OK Google, Amazon Alexa, etc. along with numerous systems that businesses apply to systematize customer service, but these are still just a way away from having the usual kinds of unscripted conversations human being have with each other.

But that may not matter when it comes to evaluating the moral influence of these kinds of technologies. Additionally, there are various applications that utilize the technology of AI. All of the information technologies like data mining, computer games, robotics, malware filtering, etc., all apply programming techniques of AI. Hence, AI will grow to be a location for the moral influence of the information technologies.

- **Artificial Life (ALife):** is known as the outgrowth of AI. ALife refers to the utilization of IT to synthesize or simulate the functions of life. The issue of describing life has been an interest in philosophy after its founding.

Mark Bedau has been outlining the philosophical inferences of ALife for some time and contends that there are two different forms of ALife and each would have a distinct moral impact if and when the separate research agendas are realized.

One kind of ALife is entirely computational, and in fact, it is the initial form of ALife studied. ALife is basically encouraged by the work of John von Neumann, a mathematician on self-replicating cellular automata which he believed would definitely lead to a computational considerate of biology as well as the life sciences (1966).

Christopher Langton (1989), the computer scientist simplified the model of von Neumann greatly and generated a simple and cellular automaton known as loops during the early eighties. He helped in getting the field off to the ground by managing the few conferences based on ALife.

ALife programs are very much unlike from AI programs. Where AI is committed on producing or improving intelligence, ALife is gratified with very simple-minded programs that show life functions instead of intelligence.

The main moral concern here is that these programs are framed to self-reproduce and in that way look like computer viruses and certainly successful ALife programs could become as malware vectors.

The second form of ALife is very much morally charged. This form of ALife is built on deploying definite biochemical and biological processes in such a way as to yield novel life forms not seen in nature.

Craig Venter introduced a public relation campaign and tried to direct the conversation regarding the issues concerned with the creation of life. In the synthesis of life, this first episode provides us a taste of controversy as well as excitement. The controversy will be created when more robust and viable artificial protocells are made.

The ethical concerns elevated by Wet ALife, as this kind of research is known are more suitably the authority of bioethics. But it does have few of the concern for us here in that Wet ALife is part of the process of turning theories from the life sciences into information technologies.

This will then tend to haze the limits between IE and bioethics. Just as software ALife might lead to risky malware, so too might Wet ALife lead to hazardous bacteria or other disease agents.

Critics recommend that there are potential moral arguments in contrast to chasing this technology and that we must use the precautionary principle here which further states that if there is an opportunity at a technology producing catastrophic harm, and there is no such scientific harmony signifying that the harm will not take place, then those who wish to develop that technology or follow that research should prove it to be innocent first.

Mark Traint and Mark Bedau argued against a tough devotion to the precautionary principle by recommending that we must go for moral daring in completing an essential step in human understanding of life.

They request to the Aristotelian notion of courage, not a foolhardy and headlong rush into the strange, but a careful and resolute step forward into the potentials provided by this research.

2.6.3. Robotics and Moral Values

Information technologies have not been gratified to restricted to software implementations and virtual worlds. These technologies are directly interacting with the generation by the application of robotics. Robotics is an evolving technology, but it has produced a huge number of uses that has significant moral implications.

Various technologies like medical robotics, personal robotics, military robotics and the world of sex robots are some of the existent applications of robotics that express the moral commitments.

The launch of semi or fully autonomous machines in the public life will not be that easy. Autonomous machines are those that take decisions with little or almost no intervention of human.

The military robotics has recognized to be one of the most ethical and charged application of robotics. These days these machines are basically operated remotely (telerobots) or semi-autonomous, but over time these machines are possible to become progressively autonomous because of the requirements of modern warfare.

In the first ten years of war in the 21st century, the robotic weaponry has been absorbed in various killings of soldiers as well as noncombatants and alone this fact is of profound moral concern. Gerhard Dabringer has done various interviews with ethicists and technologists related to the inferences of automated warfare.

2.7. INFORMATION TECHNOLOGIES OF MORALITY

A major development in the area of information technologies is that they are not just the thing of moral debates, but they are also the start to be utilized in the moral deliberation as a tool.

As AI technologies along with their applications are the type of automated issue solvers, and the moral deliberations are the type of issue, it was just a matter of time before the emergence of automated moral reasoning technologies (Figure 2.7).

Figure 2.7: Information technologies of morality.

Source: https://moraltechnologies.com.au/articles/moral-technologies-now-and-in-the-future/

Still, this is an emerging technology. It has a large number of moral implications that are quite interesting; few of them are described below. The upcoming years are probably going to see a huge number of advances in this field and the ethicists are required to pay attention to the developments as they occur.

Susan and Michael Anderson have gathered a lot of articles related to this topic in their book, *Machine Ethics* (2011), and also, Rocci Luppicini has a section of his anthology dedicated to this topic in the *Handbook of Research on Technoethics* (2009).

2.7.1. Information Technology as a Model for Moral Discovery

Patrick Grim has been a great follower of the notion that philosophy must apply different information technologies so as to illustrate and automate philosophical thought experiments.

Also, Peter Danielson (1998) has extensively written on this topic with his book *Modeling Rationality, Morality, and Evolution* with a lot of initial research in the computational theory of morality focused on utilizing computer models in order to explain the evolution of cooperation between simple software AI or ALife agents.

J. W. Sanders and Luciano Floridi argue that the information which is used in the computation theory can aid as a potential thought that can help in resolving few popular moral conundrums in philosophy, for example, the nature of evil (1999, 2001).

2.7.2. Information Technology as a Moral System

In the beginning of 20th century, John Dewey, the American philosopher proposed an inquiry theory based upon the instrumental utilization of technology. Dewey had an extensive definition of technology that further comprises machines, common tools and information systems like laws, logic, and language (Hickman, 1990).

Further, Dewey argued that nowadays people are in a kind of transactional relationship with these kinds of technologies inside which people are discovering as well as constructing the world (Hickman, 1990). This is a cooperative perspective to take as it permits the current generation to advance the idea that an IT of ethics and morality is conceivable.

As well as letting us to utterly take the idea that the transactions and relations between the human agents and those which occur between humans and their artifacts have essential ontological comparisons.

Though Dewey could just observe the upcoming revolutions in information technologies, his theories are very beneficial to the modern generation as he proposed that ethics is a kind of practice and resolving issues in ethics is similar to resolving issues in algebra. Ethics was not just a kind of theory only (Hickman, 1990).

If he is correct at his terms, then an exciting possibility evolves, such as the probability that morality and ethics are assessable issues and hence it must be possible to develop an IT that can further represent moral systems of thought.

The philosopher named as Mario Bunge in 1974, anticipated that we take the belief of a "technoethics" utterly arguing that the moral philosophers must compete with the ways the engineers deal with any issue or problem. Engineers never argue in context of reasoning by definite imperatives, but rather they utilize:

… the forms If *A* produces *B*, and you value *B*, chose to do *A*, and If *A* produces *B* and *C* produces *D*, and you prefer *B* to *D*, choose *A* rather than *C*.

In brief, the rules and regulations that have been set are basically depend on the fact and value, various researchers have submitted that this is the only path moral rules ought to be formed, specifically as rules of conduct originating from scientific statements as well as value judgments.

Briefly, ethics could be perceived as a branch of technology. Taking this notion quite seriously indicates that the process of creating information technologies is also the process of developing specific moral systems in which human, as well as artificial agents, will interact by moral transactions occasionally.

Therefore, information technologists involved in the business of establishing moral systems, whether they are aware of it or not, and whether they spire that responsibility or not.

2.8. INFORMATIONAL ORGANISMS AS MORAL AGENTS

The inclusive literature that argues in the service of the outlook of utilizing IT to develop not so moral agents is that of Luciano Floridi (1999, 2002, 2003, 2010b, 2011b), and Floridi with Jeff W. Sanders (2003).

Floridi (2010) in his researches had come up with several observations which tend to explain that, issues elevated by the ethical effects of information technologies strain all the traditional moral theories. To get rid of such rough phases, it has also been debated that what is required is a wider philosophy of information (2002).

After this move, Floridi (2003) claimed that information is an authentic environment of its own. It has its own fundamental values which are in few ways related to the natural environment and in other ways completely foreign. In either way, the consequence is that information is a thing which is worthy of moral concern on its own.

Floridi (2003) applies these notions to develop a theoretical model of moral action by utilizing the logic of object-oriented programming.

His model has seven key components:

- The moral patient *p* (or more appropriately, reagent);
- The moral agent a;
- The agent's frame of information;
- The interactions of these agents;
- The environment the interaction is happening in; and

- The factual information available to the agent regarding the condition that agent is endeavoring to navigate;
- the condition in which the interaction happens.

There is an additional literature that evaluates basic arguments like Floridi's with the expectation of growing the concept of automated moral reasoning; hence a person can speak of various automated moral technologies from very modest applications all the way to complete moral agents with the rights as well as responsibilities alike with humans.

While scholars identify that in some time developing IT would be identified as an artificial moral agent, there are enough theoretical arguments in recommending that automated moral reasoning is an ultimate possibility and thus it is a suitable area of study for those who are interested in the moral effects of information technologies.

REFERENCES

1. Francisguison's Weblog, (2009). *The-Handbook-of-Information-and-Computer-Ethic – Chapter 3: Moral Methodology and Information Technology*. [online] Available at: https://francisguison.wordpress.com/2009/04/19/the-handbook-of-information-and-computer-ethic-chapter–3-moral-methodology-and-information-technology/ [Accessed 14 Nov. 2018].
2. Hoven, J., & Weckert, J., (2008). *Information Technology and Moral Philosophy* (p. 10). [eBook]. Available at: http://assets.cambridge.org/97805218/55495/frontmatter/9780521855495_frontmatter.pdf [Accessed 14 Nov. 2018].
3. Plato.stanford.edu., (2018). *Information Technology and Moral Values (Stanford Encyclopedia of Philosophy)*. [online] Available at: https://plato.stanford.edu/entries/it-moral-values/#MorChaInfTec [Accessed 13 Nov. 2018].
4. Stahl, B., Timmermans, J., & Flick, C., (2016). Ethics of emerging information and communication technologies. *Science and Public Policy*, p. 69.
5. Ugbogbo, S., & Michael, O. A., (2016). *Ethical Issues in Information Technology* (2nd edn., p. 70). [eBook]. Available at: https://www.iuokada.edu.ng/journals/5B6AA29B40ADBA7.pdf [Accessed 13 Nov. 2018].
6. Mason, R. (1986). Four Ethical Issues of the Information Age. *MIS Quarterly*, [online] 10(1), p.5. Available at: https://www.scirp.org/(S(351jmbntvnsjt1aadkposzje))/reference/ReferencesPapers.aspx?ReferenceID=1667281 [Accessed 14 Mar. 2019].
7. Lessig, L. (2006). *CODE*. 2nd ed. [ebook] Available at: http://codev2.cc/download+remix/Lessig-Codev2.pdf [Accessed 14 Mar. 2019].
8. Floridi, L. (2003). Two Approaches to the Philosophy of Information. *Minds and Machines*, 13(4), pp.459-469.
9. E. Moore, G. (1965). Cramming more components onto integrated circuits. [ebook] Available at: http://www.monolithic3d.com/uploads/6/0/5/5/6055488/gordon_moore_1965_article.pdf [Accessed 17 Mar. 2019].
10. Floridi, L. (1999). Ethics and Information Technology, 1(1), pp.33-52.
11. Floridi, L. (2002). What is the Philosophy of Information?.

Metaphilosophy, 33(1&2), pp.123-145.

12. Floridi, Luciano. (2001). Information ethics: an environmental approach to the digital divide. Pp. 13 -22
13. Floridi, L., (2010). *The Cambridge Handbook of Information and Computer Ethics* (pp. 3–20). Cambridge: Cambridge University Press
14. Floridi, L., & Sanders, J.W. (2003). The Method of Abstraction.
15. Hickman, L. (1990). John Dewey's pragmatic technology. Bloomington u.a.: Indiana Univ. Pr.
16. Danielson, P. (1998). Modeling rationality, morality, and evolution. New York: Oxford University Press.
17. Langton, C. (1989). The proceedings of an Interdisciplinary Workshop on the Synthesis and Simulation of Living Systems. Redwood City, Calif.: Addison-Wesley.
18. P. Sullins, J. (2006). When Is a Robot a Moral Agent?. [ebook] Available at: http://www.realtechsupport.org/UB/WBR/texts/Sullins_RobotMoralAgent_2006.pdf [Accessed 17 Mar. 2019].
19. WIENER, N. (1954). *CYBERNETICS IN HISTORY*. [ebook] Available at: http://neoscenes.net/teach/cu/2012_2/atls2000_mit/pdfs/Wiener-1954-Cybernetics_in_History.pdf [Accessed 14 Mar. 2019].
20. Bostrom, N. and Sandberg*, A. (2019). *Whole Brain Emulation A Roadmap*. [ebook] Available at: https://www.fhi.ox.ac.uk/brain-emulation-roadmap-report.pdf [Accessed 17 Mar. 2019].

3

Normative Theories and Computer Ethics

CONTENTS

Information Ethics (IE) is defined as a current alternative to the traditional ethical theory to account for the moral phenomena. It is the subject of additional research to explore how it can be made to tolerate upon the practical issues and problems in Information and Communication Technologies (ICTs) and also to validate that it has a descriptive and justificatory surplus as related to the traditional ethical normative theories. Reconstructed concepts are evolved, for example, contestatory democracy, privacy as data protection, justice as fairness, function as high-level architectural principles for the design and framework of information systems and ICTs applications. The chapter deals with the branches of ethics. Mainly, it describes the normative ethical theories. Future projections are also described in the latter part of this chapter.

3.1. INTRODUCTION

ICTs are indispensable for the various economic functions in today's world. Trade, finance, transport, healthcare, science, education, administration, management, communication, energy supply, industrial production, defense, engineering, and technology; all these sectors totally rely on ICT. Extensive projects cannot be undertaken if there if there is no support from ICTs (Figure 3.1).

Figure 3.1: Computer ethics.

Source: https://www.kullabs.com/classes/subjects/units/lessons/notes/note-detail/1032

Information Societies has its share of moral problems.

- Firstly, the information should be credible and also meet the required quality standard.
- Appropriate control should be there over the Internet.
- Data processing should be done responsibly.
- Software should conform to the accepted standards.
- Personal data should be protected, and privacy should be maintained.
- There are also problems concerning the power and dominance of commercial parties.
- Information should be accessible to everyone, who wants to access. Also, information should be distributed on a fair basis.

In the twenty-first century, technology has taken over our lives. Children and young adults are the ones whom technology has influenced the most. Technology and its contents have a prolonged effect on them and have shaped their ethical values and behavioral growth.

As further technology advances, new concerns will keep arising. This issue is often discussed in public debates and attract much public attention. There is a requirement for stringent regulations because the effect technology has on lives is far-reaching. So, it is very important to have a code of conduct in place, to highlight these issues. Computer and IE have tried to do just that, in the past decades.

The features of ICTs are such that we do not have direct solutions to the ethical issues that keep arising. We cannot ignore or detach technology from our lives and have no choice, but to face all the complications and issues.

- ICTs have a universal presence and are more prevalent than our most common technical appliances. Common household artifacts and another day-to-day appliances nowadays can be called computers they are often connected through wireless network technologies. Gradually, more ordinary objects of our day-to-day life, are coming under the garb of the Internet of Things that eventually interconnects with the Internet of People. It is not easy to quantify or assess the role of technology and infrastructure on routine tasks. Their dependence on technology continues to grow but is not perceived much as technology tends to blend in the background.
- ICTs are a universal technology, because of their 'logical

malleability' (Moor, 1985). Digital computers can use a predefined set of rules to determine a result, from a set of input variables. It aids in simulation, communication, recreation, calculation, and a lot more.

They are pervasive in all fields of life and in all sectors of society. Various objects, which have been influenced on the level of the machine, are required to have an opinion regarding everything, which can get expressed and thus, stated in the form of the provided symbols.

It is not easy to find common elements in the various applications and illustrations of ICTs. The same machine can be used for weather storm simulation, for running a manufacturing unit, for distribution of electrical power in a part of a country and for archiving government information.

ICTs are a meta-technology; whose field of action is a determination of reality. The advancement and use of other technologies are dependent on ICT as it is a core ingredient in their development.

It helps us to operate machines, perform medical procedures, refine oils and transport goods over the world. It might lead to the ambiguity of the presented facts that the pertaining issues, which have been discovered to be accompanying the first- order technology are the major issues besides the meta-technology.

- ICTs are constructive technology. The process of computation of the respective technology generally tend to co- constitute all the things, on which it has been executed or implemented. ICTs can be categorized as an enabling technology. They empower us to innovate and to do old things in a novel way, by giving us fresh perspectives.

ICTs bring about a sea of change in old practices, experiences, dissertations, and relations. They usher in a new era with new practices.

ICT when used in health care, will revamp it completely, used in science and education, it will change the face of science and education, the life of the children who grow up among ICT would have a very different experience and outlook, from a person who grew up without it.

In addition to this, the information along with computer technology is, in fact, more regarding the information.

- Information is vital for everyone. Sometimes we tend to undermine its importance and how we use and process information constantly. Information is needed of planning, negotiations, decision-making, considering alternatives and judgment.

If the right information cannot be accessed, or if the information is inaccurate or incomplete, reasoning and perception are compromised. Information as well as the computer technology presented with the various techniques, so that they could be able to direct as well as deploy all the provide essential products, therefore, the major dynamics of this specified assessment, structure along with rules or regulations. Information and computer technology have also been acknowledged as the basic countenance of all the previous preferences, the rules or standards, various decisions along with moral values.

- The implementation or the execution of the information along with the communication technology have not been considered as impersonal, but generally possess the involvement of the values as well as the standards all the individuals, who have assisted in structuring or designing as well as contriving them.

Having a hold of several researches basically tends to present with the proof regarding the deliberate or unintentional establishment of all the provided standards within the respective software.

- Ultimately, the information along with the communication technology tends to gyrate across the pertaining novel objects, for instance: the software, various digital; computers as well as the products that present with the required information and thus, offers an increment to the certain novel experiences along with the practices.

This, thus, certainly tend to make it quite complex for the individuals to have an account for them, in the form of the various moral, conventional as well as the legit perceptions.

ICTs play a dominant yet perplexing role in our lives. This can be attributed the characteristics discussed above. Though it may often not be immediately clear that ICTs merit special attention, Computer, and IE aim to provide a moral assessment and scrutiny that ICTs require.

3.2. ETHICS BRANCHES

In accordance with the analytic philosophy, ethics have been segregated at the various provided stages (Figure 3.2):

- Normative ethics;

- Applied ethics; and
- Metaethics.

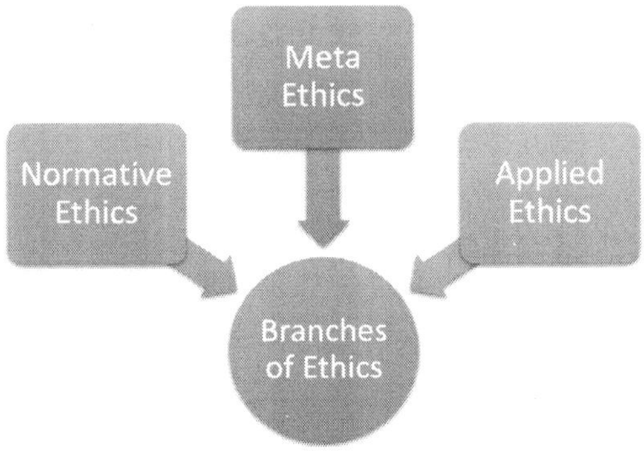

Figure 3.2: Ethics branches.

3.2.1. Meta-Ethics

The Meta-Ethics generally takes into consideration the behavior or the nature of the moral reasoning as well as the integrities. Various deliberation regarding if the ethics has been considered as relative as well as if the individuals generally tend to operate in accordance with their respective self-interest have been the great instances of the discussions related to the Meta-Ethics.

As a matter of fact, the process of designing the certain distinction based on the notions amongst the Normative Ethics, Meta-Ethics as well as the Applied or Executed Ethics, is considered to be the Meta-Ethical assessment or evaluation.

Meta-ethics is one of the fundamental branches of philosophy, which examines the nature of morality in general, and what justifies moral judgments. The three provided questions that have been scrutinized by the meta-ethics are being provided below:

- If they are true apt, are they eternally true? If it is true then what is the nature of the facts they used to represent?
- Are the ethical demands true-apt, that is, are they able to being true or not true, or are they emotional claims? and
- If there are moral truths that make them true, and they are always unquestionably true or relative to some individual, culture, or society?

In case there pertains more of facts, then the only way to seek as to what helps in making them the fact or the truth is to have an apt utilization of the value system, and thus, the main question that arises within it is whether there persists any value, which could get identified.

The various conventional philosophers are belonging to Greek culture, for instance: Plato as well as Socrates would certainly be reverting in the affirmation as they had this belief that goodness prevails, though they did not possess the identical perception regarding what all are facts and what are not.

The concept that there are no ethical truths is called "moral anti-realism." The recent pragmatist Humes possesses the place, which states that the moral countenances are basically the articulations of all the provided emotions or the feeling of mawkishness.

In actuality, the system belonging to the values related to the pertaining society, has been formed by the various great people for instance: the writers, artists, poets, leaders, and many more, or has been obtained in accordance with the provided list belonging to the moral standards or principles, for instance: moral code for the religions, wither being tacit or not (Figure 3.3).

Figure 3.3: A comparison between metaethics and normative ethics.

Source: https://opinionfront.com/metaethics-vs-normative-ethics

3.2.2. Normative Ethics

In the category of normative ethics, the major focus lies on the process of determination of the basic notion related to the ethical behavior. Various theories based on the normative ethics tend to search or discover so that they could be able to present with the action- guides; certain methods for responding to the pragmatic questions. The moral theories of Kant and Bentham are examples of normative theories that seek to provide guidelines for determining a specific course of moral action.

Certain studies based on the normative ethics provides with the problems related to how an individual is required to spend their living along with the way to perform. A theory related to normative ethics belonging to the great life generally tends to probe regarding all the pertaining needs as well as demands of the human beings so that they could be able to lead a great life.

The theory based on this study related to correct actions basically possess their major focus on searching out for the required actions that are ethically conventional in accordance with the set standard.

Alternatively, normative ethics tries to provide a system consisting of principles, procedures, and rules that can be used for determining what a person should or should not do.

A typical approach of "normative ethics" is to define "norms" as reasons to have faith in and to feel. Wherein, ultimately the theory related to the justice for the society has been considered as a trial for seeking the way as to how the society is required to get designed or structured, as well as how to disperse or distribute the goods of society related to the power as well as independence, within the pertaining society.

3.2.3. Applied Ethics

Within this specified category of ethics, the major focus is to cope with the specified facets of the actions performed by the human beings as well as to describe the basic prospects related to the procedure of having a discussion grounded on the various issues, which may get aroused within those respected facets or aspects.

It has been acknowledged as the core branch of ethics, which tends to pursue the process of probing the implementation or the execution of the theories based on the ethics in the actuality. To its conclusion, the applied ethics tends to highlight the probability of the incongruity regarding the manner under which all the principles or standards, as well as the pertaining theories, are required to get implemented.

Major areas of applied ethics are listed below:

- Bioethics;
- Medical ethics;
- Public sector ethics;

- Business ethics;
- Welfare ethics;
- Legal ethics (justice) Media ethics;
- Decision-making ethics;
- Computer ethics;
- Environmental ethics;
- Automation ethics;
- Manufacturing ethics;
- Robot ethics.

The rigorous deontological principles based on the form or type of 10 provided commandments presents with certain explanations to the specified cases, which are not being considered as conventional or acceptable at an international level.

For instance, in case of the medical ethics, an approach related to the rigorous deontology would never be provided with the consent to the dishonesty of the provide patient regarding their respective disorder. In comparison to this, the approach belonging to the utilitarianism might provide with its permit to the process of lying to the respective patients, only in case if the results of that specific dishonesty if for their well- being.

3.3. NORMATIVE ETHICAL THEORIES

The term normative has been considered as an adjective that has been generated from the word, which basically means a set principle or a regulation. Therefore, the norms based on the morality or the ethics with the help of which, the individuals are assumed to have a sound observation.

Public perception of these standards varies; hence, the various normative theories of ethics emphasize on what they claim makes an action a moral action: on what things are good or bad, and what kind of behavior is right as opposed to the wrong (Figure 3.4).

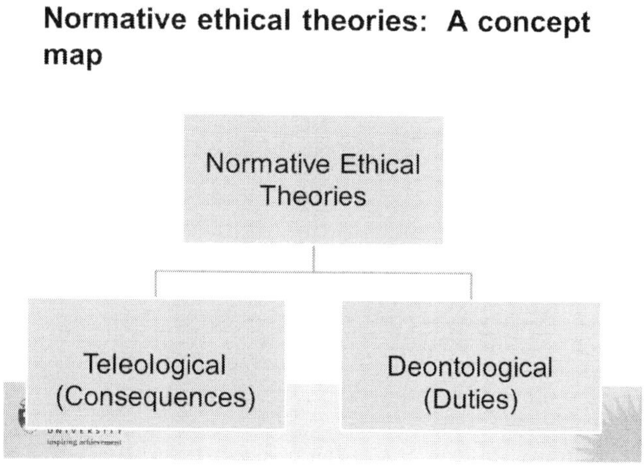

Figure 3.4: Major normative ethical theories.

Source: https://slideplayer.com/slide/10296472/

Two normative theories are discussed in this chapter. They explain three different sets of ideas about ways of ethical living.

3.3.1. Deontological Theory

The terminology of deontology has been generated out of the Greek Deon, which means the responsibility or the compulsions, essentiality as well as with the process of binding. In general, such words, when get translated, turn out be as a duty, so the various theories that are grounded on the deontology try to establish what one's moral duties are. Once these moral duties have been enumerated, those duties are the foundation of moral 'rules.'

Deontological systems emphasize that the primary focus should be on confirming to duties and rules because that is where the moral worth of an action lies. Evaluating the consequences of the action is secondary.

Kant would have argued that for an action to be considered as moral, extrinsic reasons, such as personal gains, should be negated and the action should be done solely as an obedience to a rule. In his example, Kant explains, a grocer cannot be called as kind, if he is good to his customer, just to earn their loyalty.

If he does consider being kind, his moral duty, any moral goodness of his action is negated. The grocer should not have an ulterior motive and should be kind because of its intrinsic goodness. It can be deduced that ethics based on the deontological possess the capability of leading the various individuals to perform in the manner, which tends to bring in the negative repercussions.

3.3.2. Consequential Theory

According to the Consequentialist theories of ethics, consequence of an action should be the basis to judge the moral worth of an action. Thus, in case of an action, being good or bad is generally the one, which helps in generating the great conclusions in totality, within the specified condition.

There are, therefore situations where a consequentialist would be prepared to lie if that was thought necessary to bring about the best consequence(s).

The theory that is grounded on the repercussions and that too well- known, is Utilitarianism that has been acknowledged as the great instance of the act- consequentialism, wherein all the correct actions have been considered as those, which helps in maximizing the pleasure of the perceptive beings, which means that all the individuals who can reason, feel, think as well as possess an experience.

In comparison to this, the theories which are based on the deontology usually tend to possess their major concentration on the essential or important value belonging to the rule itself, within the ethics belonging to the consequences, the major focus is on the basic importance of such repercussions of the provided rule. No act can be categorically termed as right or wrong.

3.3.3. Teleological Theory

The term "Teleological" is derived from the Greek word "telos," which means 'goal,' 'end' or 'purpose.' This word is already known to the people in relation with the Design Argument for the presence of God, which is also called as the Teleological Argument, as it claims that the purpose of God is visible in what is observed about the universe.

Within ethics, the basic conclusion, the objective or the generic reasoning, which all the researchers generally tend to find has been referred to as the provided obligations which are required in the process of achieving the specified objectives based on the morality or the ethics or the end results.

For the theories based on the teleological ethics, thus, in case one required to seek for the way as to how one should be conducting oneself in accordance with respect to the morality or ethics, then that person is required to make a decision as to what all objects they should be possessing in terms of the ethics. Such theories can also be considered as consequentialist and thus are being headed in the direction of the set objectives or the goals or the specified purpose, a theory based on the teleology, might also consider to have an achievement of the great repercussions in any of the provided condition. This will follow the simple reason that to achieve the best consequence in any particular situation will generally contribute to the overall goal.

3.3.4. Character-Based Theory

Many of the researchers have observed that the various theories based on the repercussions as well as the deontology are basically act-centered, and thus, they tend to label them as the specified acts, being positive or negative, correct or wrong.

Being a dissimilarity to this, the ethics or the morality which is based on the character, is considered to be agent-centered that means that the righteousness is not just pertaining within the act but within that specified person, wherein the researchers tend to label or observe them if the agent is a great or honorable person in accordance with their respective habits as well as by their character.

In the theory of Kant, a person doing good acts morally by habit is not considered as good morally, as the moral goodness needs the moral agent to resolve what should be done in accordance with the reason.

Having a consideration of an instance: there pertained a eulogy regarding a lady, some years back, in one of the provided communities belonging to the church, who had been addressed as being the most honorable person as she was good to everyone, habitually, in spite of judging them for who they are.

3.4. PROFESSIONAL ETHICS

The ethics belonging to the business or the corporate world presents with the advice regarding the connection between the various experts or the professionals in a way that they could be able to assist each other as well as the entire pertaining society in the way which is best suited, without the possession of any fear of the other professionals that tends to weaken them with the actions that are considered to be less ethical (Figure 3.5).

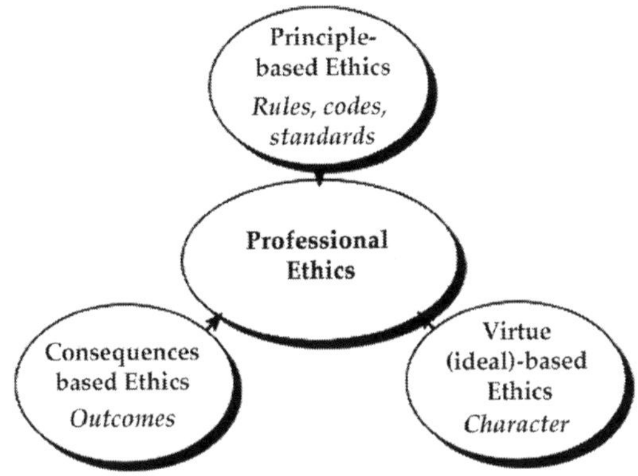

Figure 3.5: Professional ethics.

Source:https://www.journalofnursingregulation.com/article/S2155–8256(15)30232–5/fulltext

Codes similar to these are being accessible in various professions, and thus, are considered to be distinct from that of the moral codes that were supposedly utilized within the academics as well as the religion of the whole of the extensive society.

Ethical codes are more specialized than moral codes, more internally consistent, and typically simple to be applied by an ordinary practitioner of the profession, without the need for extensive interpretation.

The Hippocrates Oath is one of the most primitive codes of professional ethics that provided rules for the ethical performance of the physician so as not to harm their parents. The oath, as well as the complete code, is written in the first person.

The recent professional codes possess the identical characteristics or the attributes, presenting with the specification as to what all will be the pre-dominant responsibilities as well as to whom the professional possesses, as clearly or tacitly as possible.

Below are some of the examples related to the codes:

- The code of the Institute of Electrical and Electronic Engineers (IEEE);
- The code of the National Society of Professional Engineers (NSPE);
- The code for robotics engineers developed by the Worcester Polytechnic Institute (WPI);

- The code of the American Society for Mechanical Engineers (ASME).

3.5. NORMATIVE RELATIVISM THEORY

The theory based on the normative relativism has contended that all the perceptions, which are based on the morality or the ethics, for instance: all the standards, values along with the virtues have been considered as equivalently legit.

This theory has an inherent contradiction. As per this theory, there are no universal norms, but the theory uses a universal norm. This is the main drawback of this theory. It tends to make any of the discussions grounded on the ethics quite impossible.

This is a philosophical theory that is NOT well supported by the evidence gathered by cultural anthropologists, nor could science support a theory about the past and future! It is a theory that has evidence against it.

3.5.1. Factors Contributing Towards the Popularity of Normative Relativism Theory

Various factors that tend to have a contribution within the admiration of the theory based on the normative ethical relativism have been provided below:

- It is apparent that moral rules and laws differ in different countries. Laws that apply to people of one country cannot be binding on people of another country.

People around the globe, belong to different ethnicities, follow different customs and hence have a different perspective of what is right and what is wrong. It is impractical to have a universal moral standard that will be binding on all people around the world.

- Increased compassion and acceptance among people, of different values and beliefs as well as the requirement to have an aversion of the harms belonging to the ethnocentrism. Thus, the basic longing to have an acceptance as well as to laud the beauty along with the values of the world, which is being considered as multi-cultured.
- The disappointment for many of the people is to possess a thought that there could have been a third substitute to the autocracy of the

morality or the ethics that have been linked or connected with the provided religion along with the relativism of the specific culture.

Thus, the Sophists possessed the belief that all the of the pertaining societies generally tend to create their own respective rules as well as them persists none of the rules that have been accepted globally, no gods are there to rule as well as make or create rules.

3.5.2. Challenges Related to Normative Relativism Theory

There pertain various issues along with the criticism belonging to the theory, which is based on the relativism of the normative ethics or morality, which are:

- As per this theory, there are no common criteria across the globe to judge moral and ethical issues.

It is only a good thing in those cultures where it is promoted.

It cannot be promoted for all peoples.

Whereas, there are other countries where people have been inculcated with the belief that they are superior and possess the right to dominate and exploit other people. Therefore, that group of people will not perceive tolerance as a virtue.

- In accordance with the theory based on the relativism of the normative ethics, each of the culture possesses its own respective notions or thoughts regarding the morality as well as ethics. The Theory of Normative Ethical Relativism is not capable of supporting or explaining criticisms of the majority's opinions by minorities.
- In case, this specified theory has been implemented on the various distinctive cultures as they have been cultivated in a very distinct environment of the society, then, it will certainly be applied on the individuals that have been grown apart them.
- The theory belonging to the relativism of the normative ethics generally tend to act as a generic experience along with the various notions based on the ethics along with the morality.

Even individuals who claim that they believe that the Theory of Normative Ethical Relativism is precise do make moral decisions regarding the practices of people in different cultures. For example, they do condemn female infanticide and genital mutilation and several other practices, even practices that go back many centuries.

3.6. VALUE PLURALISM

Christine Korsgaard has specified that one of the major attributes of the humanity is our close as well as bottomless capability for consulting the values. It is not due to the shared values which must grant consideration to one-another but due to shared capacity shared capability for conferring value.

In the other terms, the basic datum regarding the behavior or nature of the respective human beings is generally that part, which usually tends to make the varied liberal forms or types of the democracy belonging to the state, the correct ones.

This fact about human beings and human lives has served as a point of departure of much of contemporary moral theorizing. We confer value on different things, but we also confer different values on the same thing.

In accordance with the distinct context, many of the countries have utilized the conventional proverb regarding the various distinctions that are pertaining between the hedgehog as well as the fox, so that they could be able to have an illustration or description regarding the dissimilarity between the pluralists along with the monists, for instance: the hedgehog possess the potentiality of having a sight of just a single huge object, whereas the fox holds the capability of witnessing more of small things.

Various contemporary moral philosophers observe different small things in spite of one big thing while looking closely at morality and ethics: Thomas Nagel, Bernard Williams, Amartya Sen, and Martha Nussbaum, Joseph Raz, John Rawls, Robert Audi (2007) are few of the most renowned – all defended forms of value pluralism. Endeavors, social relationships, and human lives are intricate and variegated.

Various issues with which all the people are supposed to get encountered are the multitudinous or the variedness, their respective actions or functions possess several repercussions as well as a wide range or variety of the impacts on the other individuals.

Individuals possess the potentiality of witnessing or perceiving distinctive things in accordance with the entirely distinctive viewpoint or opinion.

They also can have a record of the outcome of their respective actions along with the mechanism of their activities, they possess the capability of grasping distinctive things in accordance with their specified perceptions and thus, can discover or recognize as well as commiserate with all the other individuals that are their near and dear ones, or with the individuals that are far away.

They might consider their respective condition along with the perception from oblivion, or they can perceive the world according to their own viewpoints, without just having thinking as to one's point of view is way more important in comparison to that of the others.

Such perceptions, as well as the values, are considered to be all egalitarian, wherein all the other distinctive things remain equivalent.

Therefore, it cannot be the situation that outcomes or consequences and the extension of happiness, utility, and pleasure are the only thing that counts from the moral perspective. Nor can it be the case that compliance with one formal moral principle of duty and human dignity can be the only right making criterion, whatever tire consequences.

Even a request or plead to the values belonging to the perfectionist or the expert as to how a perfect or an ideal individual is required to behave, for instance: about some of the matters related to the sex or the personal sanitation as well as the aesthetics, which might be having a possession of the prior likelihood or conceivability, but they are generally being dominated in all the cases that are grounded on the conflicts with the process of utilization or the generic access or rights.

Distinctive theories based on the normative ethics along with the conventions or the traditions, have segregated a single kind or form of the value, symbolized or exemplified it and thus, simultaneously modulated the essentiality of the other values, then downplayed it to the prior worth or value of the preference, or might have removed them in a single go.

Monistic opinions of the moral theory assume that all a person desires to know is one value or one simple principle that expresses it.

Thus, in order to retain one believe that there persists a single value of expert, which tends to act as a blockage for all the other values, be it the dignity of the human being or the process of maximizing the consumption or utility of the goods, booming period for the human beings or the self-interests, generally results in the overt narrow sight of the criticality related to the issues of morality as well as draining of the condition belonging to the human beings that are supposed to get ignored, specifically in the case of the applied ethics, which always tries to be as pertinent as possible to the process of evaluation of the technologies along with the process of making of the public policies.

Ethics may be related to the praise as well as blame, prescription or evaluation, conflict resolution, action guidance, character traits and virtues, the logic of permission and obligation, basic needs and human rights, utility, consequences, and outcomes, well-being, money, ideals, principles, duties, capabilities, duties, and responsibilities, values, interest, and preferences.

It thus might be regarding the extensively generic or the global facts or regarding the acknowledgments, which are specified to the notions. In accordance with the presented condition, any of such notions, as well as the vocabularies, can get highly utilized.

To foreclose the use of them with their associated background views in favor of one seems unduly restrictive and reductive in practical matters.

3.7. MORAL THEORY

3.7.1. Primacy of Practice

Ethics or morality has been considered as a division of the pragmatic philosophy and therefore, has been principally solicitous regarding the pragmatic issues along with the provided actions.

The main objective of the argumentation based on the ethics or morality, reasoning of such ethics as well as justified judgment has been considered as the coherent explanation as well as the process of settling of all the pertaining clashes and discrepancies, as to who all are interested in becoming, what all they are supposed to do, the process of refraining the self- interest, along with the enhancement of collaboration as well as serene cohabitation of all the respective creatures, which are considered to be perceptive, within a mutual or communal environment.

The thinking based on the ethics or morality provides with an indication to the various reasons so that they could be able to restrain the behavior of the self- interest as well as the strategies related to the process of self-serving.

People reflect upon and try to advance their moral ideas and beliefs with the end in opinion of getting answers to the question that how to act, decide, and select in such a way so as to follow their own happiness without interrupting with the similar quest of others and how to lead a prosperous life.

The key objective in the facet of the ethics is not just to incorporate the generic theory along with the great set of undying fact but also to present with the solutions or the explanations with their respective reasoning as well as the elucidations to all the pertaining issues that are pragmatic in nature.

The researchers generally tend entangle themselves in the theory based on ethics so that they could be able to have a creation or the formation of the various rational or knowledgeable resources, which possess the capability of assisting them in the process of having a determination of all the believes grounded on the ethics, which are considered to be valuable of their promotions.

They had this perception that all the pertinent philosophies generally tend to get recovered whenever it concludes to be acting similar to that of the device in order to be coping with the pertaining issues belonging to the philosophers and thus, turns out to be procedure that has been refined by the respective philosophers, in order to tackle the varied issues of the men.

3.7.2. Theoretical Pluralism

Value pluralism has various inferences in context of ethical theory. First is, different theories and the core values may apprehend various relative features of the particular case morally, without essentially leading to correct and unique answers.

Moreover, as there pertains various distinctive frameworks based on the notions or the contexts as well as the vocabularies that have been considered as accessible so that they could be able to explain distinct conditions, wherein each of them might be providing with the altered explanation to the existing questions grounded on the salience along with its pertinence, and thus, it might direct to the process of enunciation of the varied, distinctive sets related to the questions based on the moralities or ethics.

The individuation and description of concrete cases has implications for what is subsumed under a general moral rule, principle or theory. In general, it is also being acknowledged as the issue or problem of all the pertinent explanations.

Much of the researchers have discovered that the act-token would certainly be falling under the category of the major probable standards or the principles belonging to the actions, which usually tends to make it quite complex for them to provide with an answer as to what all descriptions of the act has been considered as pertinent for the evaluation of the morality or ethics.

Onora O'Neill asks in the discussion of Anscombe's problem, that 'should we evaluate an action under the account that an agent aims it or under descriptions, others think salient, or under descriptions that has noted by nobody?'

Few may define it as "aiding a friend," few as illegally replicating the program of a software or as offending a law that is accepted morally to achieve some benefits.

3.8. THE IMPACT OF GLOBALIZATION AND THE INTERNET ON COMPUTER ETHICS

Due to the influence or the effect of the process of computation in the past recent years on the world, as well as due to the process of convergence of the computation as well as the technologies related with the communications, which has happened in the recent times, the basic facet of the ethics grounded on the information as well as the communication technology, might have been apprehended in the form of one that is recently being in the condition of the change or the flux.

Others such as van den Hoven, Johnson, Introna, and Nissenbaum (1999) have utilized the expression "Information and Communications Technology Ethics" or ICT Ethics to try to abduct the conjunction of communications-related and information-related ethical issues in a global context.

To date, there is no clear agreement on what new label should be used to describe the field; nor, for that matter, is there agreement that a new label is needed.

Recently, few authors have started using the expressions such as 'Internet Ethics' and 'Cyber Ethics' in ways that might be construed by some to infer that the Internet has created modern ethical issues and that perhaps a distinct field of study devoted to ethical issues concerning this relatively new medium is required.

Clearly, the Internet has perpetuated and, in certain cases, exacerbated many of the ethical issues associated with the use of earlier computing technologies.

Though Nissenbaum properly specified the limitations of normative theories of privacy in context of protecting the privacy in public, few might conclude from Nissenbaum's analysis that the internet, being a "public space," grants us with a modern set of privacy concerns.

In spite of the various challenges pertaining that has been imposed by the internet in accordance with the concern related to the security of the various kinds of private information, wherein there persists none of the persuasive proofs providing any positive response on the novel issues related to privacy has been announced with the help of the respective intermediary or that one might possess the requirement regarding the novel group related to the privacy on the cyberspace.

Comparatively, it does not seem to be a substantial argument for the claim that a different area of "internet ethics" is either required.

3.9. FUTURE PROJECTIONS

In this, the major focus would be on the manner with which the process of globalization, as well as the advancement of the Internet technologies, possessed an impact on the recent or the modern discussion within the ethics belonging to the information as well as the communication technology.

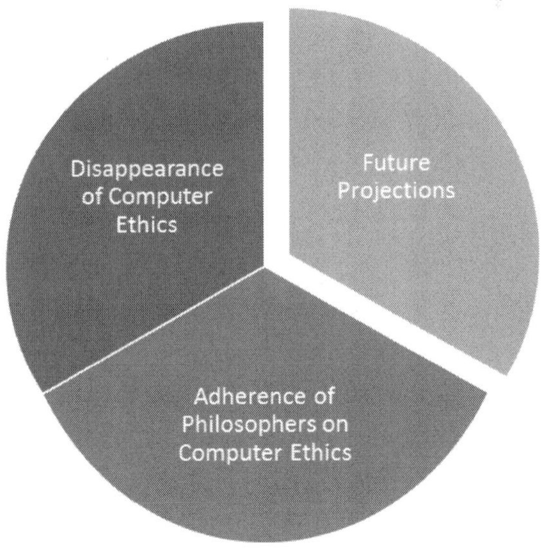

Figure 3.6: Future projections.

However, the major issue related to this is to have an exact detail regarding the impact of the continuation of the global interaction or relation as well as the advancement or the varied innovations within the technology on the fortune of the facet or domain belonging to the ethics related to information as well as communication technology.

Some have already put forth explicit hypotheses, while others have speculated informally about the future of the field. The basic enticing perspective regarding the fortune has been described by various researchers, including Deborah Johnson (1999) (Figure 3.6).

3.9.1. Will Computer Ethics 'Disappear' in the Future?

Johnson recommended that the area of computer ethics may or should disappear in the coming future. She assumes that whatever we are considering as issues in computer ethics may become well integrated into the "ordinary ethics" issues.

Johnson has been considered as very cautious while pointing out or indicating that the issues or the problems are not going to get mitigated on their own, instead they are not even going to get manipulated or posed similar to the of the problems or issues related to the ethics belonging to the information along with the communication technologies.

He argued that the computer technology tends to mend or affect the actions performed by the human beings in varied ways in which it has never been implemented or executed. Nevertheless, in case a novel execution or the application has been established within the process of moral thinking, it generally tends to become the potential conditions based on the various contexts.

And, as soon as the various researchers were about to have an assumption regarding the computer technology, being one of the major parts of the world that they are living in, he presented with the prediction that the ethics or the morality of the information and communication technology is most likely to get vanished.

Then, the major question arouses as if the predictions made by Johnson, worth the laud or not. When considered from the vantage point of the cluster of computer ethics issues involving privacy, security, property, and free speech, her speculation about the future of the field would seem fairly cogent.

Nevertheless, as computing becomes a part of presumed background condition, privacy issues comprising computing would not observe to be significantly distinct in nature from the privacy issues in general.

But when it got sighted in accordance with the perceptions of the ethics or morality associated with the information and communication technology, being a track for the ethics belonging to the experts or the professionals or being the basic division related to the philosophy, grounded on the applied ethics, the positions held by Johnson could get challenged.

Some of the individuals, who were in support of this specified perception, having an inclusion of the practitioners of the computer sciences, for instance: Gotterbarn (1991), would certainly be responding to the forecasting or the prediction made by Johnson, by presenting with an indication regarding the various problems or issues being associated with it, having an involvement of the certain responsibilities for the provided experts or the professionals, who are operating within the facet of the computers would certainly not being distant in accordance with the future, ethics belonging to the computers will not be going away, for instance: the facet or the field belonging to the ethics being associated with the professionals.

But then, another question arises related to the ethics belonging to the information as well as the communication technology being the branch of the applied ethics.

Antonio Marturano (2000) has lately provided with the response to Johnson through a demand regarding the two pertaining ways with which she could be able to understand or interpret the claim made by her regarding the banishment of the computer ethics:

- As an autonomous discipline, computer ethics will disappear; and
- As an aspect of applied ethics, computer ethics will disappear.

In addition to challenges posed to Johnson's prediction by Gotterbarn and Marturano, others would also likely disagree with Johnson.

It would surely appear that questions related to AI comprising moral responsibility will endure to rise in the coming future and that these AI related questions would benefit arguably from the analysis by computer ethicists.

Rather, it is believed that a better knowledge of how computer technology has emerged during the last fifty years can aid to recognize more clearly some of the issues and challenges that people will face in the future when they attain a state of more comprehensive 'technological convergence.'

In considering the impact that computing has had for ethics during the last half of the twentieth century, we could view it from the vantage point of four distinct stages or phases.

In case of the phase 1, belonging to 1950s as well as 1960s, the technology of the computers generally tends to have an inclusion of mainly the extensive mainframes of the provided computers that were supposedly no associated or not connected machines, or in the other words: the stand-alone machine.

Certain repercussions associated with the morality of the process of computation of all the concerns related to the society as well as morality, at this specified facet that can be viewed in the form of the various questions that in today's time, are being linked or connected with the artificial intelligence (AI).

During this phase, the other concern was the fear linked with "Big Brother," as it is a centralized government that could collect substantial amount of information regarding its citizens. This information is stored in large databases indefinitely in the form of electronic records.

Having a consideration of the phase 2, belonging to the 1970s as well as 1980s, the first and the foremost step for this is to initiate with the viewing up of the idea of merging the devices related to communication as well as various machines for the process of computation or calculation, presenting with a progress to the epoch belonging to the information or the computer networks.

Within this specified facet, various personal computers, mainframes, microcomputers as well as the minicomputers could all get associated or connected with the help of the networks of the computer that has been held privately, in the format of the LANs (i.e., local area networks) as well as WANs (i.e., wide area networks).

Information could now be readily exchanged between databases, which were accessible to networked computers.

The beginning of internet technology enhances amongst different other things, anonymity, concerns linked with free speech, trust, authority, and so on, that evolve during this phase of computing technology.

In addition to this, there pertain varied questions, which are of greater concern, related to the personal information, possessing private character or the personal one that can be simply accessible on the cyberspace.

At present, we are on the threshold of what could be called Phase 4, in which we are beginning to experience an unprecedented level of convergence of technologies. At the phase 3 the interface to and the metaphor of, computing technology is yet same as the previous phases such as screen, keyboard, etc. and the computers are yet considered as something peripheral to the people that is, they are external devices that can be humans use to interact.

As it is quite known that the computers have become nearly omnipresent in today's world, and, thus, too much of extent a part of what the individuals are as the human beings, feasibly, it can be said the people are on the verge of the novel, as well as debatably extensively considerable epoch of the process of merging.

Certainly, it may turn out to be problematic to disperse out convinced aspects of the biology from the technology in the near future.

Because of the situation, it is envisaged that in Phase 4, it may seem that a view that fits with Johnson's conception (described above), where computer ethics as a separate field of study will go away. In the exact opposite to this, it has been assumed that there will be an extensive requirement for both facet of the ethics belonging to the information as well as the communication technologies along with the philosophers so that they could be able to do research on that specified track, in comparison to the previous times.

3.9.2. Why Should Philosophers Continue to do Computer Ethics?

Prior to the process of trying to provide an explanation to the questions as to why all the philosophers are required to perform the ethics being associated with the information as well as the communication information, it would certainly be considered as helpful in presenting with an essential differentiation in accordance with the perspective of Johnson regarding the fortune of the specified track. Two points have been described below that possess the worth of getting considered individually:

- Computer ethics may vanish in the future; and
- Computer ethics should vanish in the future.

In the future, certain problems being linked with the technology, being one of the prospects, would certainly be continuing to pressurize as well as extend the theory based on the morality or the ethics as well as being persistent in the process of introducing varied confusions as well as the muddles grounded on the various contexts or the notions.

In both the areas, philosophers will be required to provide help. Many of the researchers have already taken into consideration certain ways with which, the philosophers have provided with their respective reverts to the pertaining problems or the issues, possessing an involvement of the requirement to have an assessment along with the revision of the various theories, based on ethics, so that they could be able to inscribe the pertaining issues.

Let us next examine some areas in which philosophers can help to clarify some existing and future conceptual confusions associated with moral issues in computing.

Birrer goes on to specify that through various issues considered in the strained sense of computer ethics may even be normative; they are not essentially ethical in nature. Regrettably, such an essential differentiation has been often gone through, or in various cases, has been completely unnoticed, within the much of the literature related to the morality of the information as well as the communication technologies.

Philosophers can also continue to help refine our understanding of many of the standard computer ethics issues, e.g., issues involving privacy, property, crime, and so forth as these concepts become stretched and strained by changing technological innovations.

In the various previous parts of this specific chapter, an instance regarding the privacy with respect to the cyberspace, has already been defined so that they could be able to provide with an illustration regarding some of the pertaining muddles as to if there persists any of the novel of the rare issues related with the ethics or morality that has been introduced by the provided technology.

Let us now consider a different issue related to computer ethics, viz., crime comprising computer technology, to demonstrate few ways in which philosophers can help to reduce some conceptual confusions.

Confusions regarding the distinction of crimes that should or should not be considered, as a computer crime will probably become more intensified, and the devices of communication remain to merge.

Many of the researchers have observed that the generic crime, possessing an involvement of the varied cell phones, is somehow being associated with cloning i.e., the process of reprogramming the cell phone of an individual to transmit the digits of the mobile belonging to the other individual or party, so that the party, which is supposedly innocent, would be charged for all the calls that have not been made by that specified individual or the party.

Should we classify this particular criminal act as a form of computer crime or Cybercrime on the grounds that digital technology was involved in the criminal act? A question has been raised as to what will happen at the time of the occurrence of the I-phones or the internet phones, which are considered to be a great convergence of the digital telephony along with the net. And, how will all the crimes, possessing an involvement of the convergence of the advanced technologies, would be able to get understood or supported.

Thus, philosophers can aid to reduce various confusions that will be the outcome of technology convergence in the future.

Obviously, some of the provided critics would certainly be asking for as to why all the pertaining philosophers are required to devote their respective time in the process of discussion as well as the assessment or the evaluation of the varied persistent questions, having an involvement of the fortune related with the advancement in the technology of computers.

The best explanation to that question has been described by Moor (1998c) when he provided with the apt remarks as: "If philosophers do not confront the conceptual and ethical problems of the internet, who will?"

REFERENCES

1. Hoven, J., (n.d.). *Information and Computer Ethics* (p. 20). [eBook]. Available at: https://d1rkab7tlqy5f1.cloudfront.net/TBM/Over%20faculteit/Afdelingen/Values%2C%20Technology%20and%20Innovation/People/Full%20Professors/The_use_of_normative_theories_in_computer_ethics.pdf [Accessed 14 Nov. 2018].
2. Normative ethical theories. (n.d.). *Hodder Education Draft* (p. 25). [eBook] Available at: https://www.hoddereducation.co.uk/media/Documents/RS/4_Normative_ethical_theories_Natural_moral_law.pdf [Accessed 14 Nov. 2018].
3. Schiaffonati, V., (2018). *Computer Ethics: Normative Ethics – Ethical Theories* (p. 27). [eBook]. Available at: http://home.deib.polimi.it/schiaffo/CE/normative%20ethics%204.pdf [Accessed 14 Nov. 2018].
4. Tavani, H., (2001). *The State of Computer Ethics as a Philosophical Field of Inquiry: Some Contemporary Perspectives, Future Projections, and Current Resources* (p. 12). [eBook] Netherlands: Kluwer Academic Publishers, Available at: https://static1.squarespace.com/static/52095f5de4b0bc18c96d1924/t/57d434cc15d5db80ead8f8c7/1473524941420/Tavani+-+2001+-+The+state+of+computer+ethics+as+a+philosophical+field+of+inquiry+Some+contemporary+perspectives%2C+future+projections%2C+and.pdf [Accessed 14 Nov. 2018].
5. G. Johnson, D. (1999). *Sorting Out the Uniqueness of Computer-Ethical Issues*. [ebook] Available at: https://core.ac.uk/download/pdf/41174283.pdf [Accessed 17 Mar. 2019].
6. Moor, T., Raisch, J. and O'Young, S. (1998). Discrete Event Dynamic Systems. Discrete Event Dynamic Systems, 12(1), pp.83-107. Marturano, A. (2000). Media ethics. Regulating the Information Society. Milano: F. Angeli.
7. Gotterbarn, D. (1991). Computer Ethics: Responsibility Regained. [online] Cscietsu.edu. Available at: https://csciwww.etsu.edu/gotterbarn/artpp1.htm [Accessed 17 Mar. 2019].
8. Van Den Hoven, J., Introna, L. D., Johnson, D. G., & Nissenbaum, H. (1999). Ethics and Information Technology: Editorial. Ethics and Information Technology, 1(1), 1-3.

9. Audi, R. (2007). Moral value and human diversity. New York: Oxford University Press.
10. MOOR, J. (1985). WHAT IS COMPUTER ETHICS?. Metaphilosophy, 16(4), pp.266-275.

4

Ethical Issues in the Information and Computer Sector

CONTENTS

The field of information technology (IT) and digitization have expanded to unrestricted boundaries, and there is no stopping this field from growing even further. These are something's, though, that need to be curtailed as they have resulted in the degrading value of the field. Ethics have always been an important subject in any field that humanity has taken up, to ensure that humans do not indulge themselves in activities that degrade the value of the subject. In the field of IT and computer systems; also, there have been various ethical issues that concern individuals and their personal lives. In this chapter, the readers get an insight various such issues and get to understand the flaw in the computing systems.

4.1. INTRODUCTION

The world that the people live in is ever evolving and ever-changing in terms of technological innovations and developments. In such a world, it is bound to be that the subject of ethical issues is brought up from time to time. This subject requires great concern and seeks the support of people in the form of best efforts they can put in to resolve the issues with ethics (Figure 4.1).

Figure 4.1: Ethics form an integral part of computer systems.

Source:https://cdn.pixabay.com/photo/2017/03/02/07/32/ethics–2110589_960_720.jpg

Among the most discussed issues regarding the IT industry, the ones related to information communication technologies, it has generally come up on the top. The uncontrolled expansion of the ICT and its overwhelming use that support the technology structure across industries have made some notable impacts on the social existence of people which makes it a subject that gets enough attention from the ethical point of view.

The problems regarding this have been discussed in such a manner that the confusion regarding it has had varied impacts in the society. The various issues that the use of ICT gives birth to are a breach of privacy of a person or an organization, taking over the rights of property, pricking the various social rights of the people, and the accountability that sets up due to the situations that take place after the use of ICTs.

The issues that have been mentioned above have given rise to other related problems such as unemployment, improper working conditions and degrading a person's individuality. However, the actions and measures that must have been taken up to resolve these issues and problems have not been up to the mark. As Fielden has stated in 2004, the field of IT serves as a center point and is employed across almost all the industrial verticals like commercial sector, governmental organizations, pharmaceutical sector, education, entertainment business, industrial setups, thus concerning the whole society in a specific way.

The benefits of IT industry do not need an extra introduction. But, just like the other evolving sectors, the use of IT also carries with itself certain flaws and implications that affect the society in some way or the other. It contributes to the issues related to ethics in three main ways, which may also be termed as ethical issue. They are:

- Personal Privacy;
- Access Right; and
- Harmful Actions.

When the subject is about the personal privacy, IT may help in exchanging large amounts of information from anyone or from any place across the globe and at any point of time. This kind of exchange gives rise to an increased risk of having the data leaked and having the privacy of an entity breached. This makes it essential for the humans to take steps in order to maintain the privacy and honor the quality of data that concerns different people. This incorporates the measures needed to make sure that the data remains accurate, and additionally securing it from being accessed by an unauthorized entity or getting the information disclosed accidentally to the people who are not meant to have it.

The other part of the issues regarding ethics is the right to access the content.

The matter of security in the digital space has shifted from being one of the low priorities to that of a highly prioritized one on the board of agenda of the different institutions and organizations in charge. This has happened because of the sudden rise in the online market of the international trade.

The subject matter has been even more in the focus of late owing to the digital breach of the security at some significant organizations such as the Los Alamos National Laboratories and NASA in the United States. In the recent times, there have been numerous incidents of the illegal breach attempts by the hackers into the administrative systems of the US government. The connections on the internet network cannot be a cent percent vulnerability proof unless the policies and strategies regarding the security of digital platforms are thoroughly established and practiced.

4.2. FOUNDATIONAL ISSUES IN INFORMATION ETHICS

There are specific questions that are pointed at the uniqueness of information ethics (IE). There have been numerous arguments given by the researchers and various other people who have studied about the subject in favor of IE and its study claiming the field to hold theoretical importance. Following this kind of research and study, the digital world and its utilization lead to certain obstacles that are meta-ethical, epistemic, and ethical in nature. These hurdles authorize solving the issues in the form of unified classes that need specific training and perfection.

On the one hand, where the researchers and publishers contend that IE holds its uniqueness in a theoretical and essential way, the other way around they tend to be divided on the way they consider it to be distinct.

4.2.1. Interpreting the Uniqueness Thesis

The uniqueness thesis is interpreted in different ways. In a first way, the people may put a point forward that the ethics regarding computers is different from others in a way that some of the activities that the digital world involves, requires the ethical qualities that may not be borne in any other kind of sector.

4.2.2. The Meta-Ethical Thesis

There are acts in computer ethics that cannot adequately be characterized by the traditional concepts of obligatory, permissible, good, and supererogatory. The meta-ethical thesis, then, makes the very strong claim that the very meta-ethical foundation for general and applied ethical thinking is inadequate.

On the other hand, the researchers may contend that the theories regarding ethics that are present currently may prove to be enough to find solutions to the problems concerning certain areas of applied ethics, but turn inadequate to find solutions to the issues engaging the use of computers. Hence, IE is different in certain ways.

4.2.3. The Normative Thesis

Computer technologies lay down ethical issues that cannot, as a neutral matter, be sufficiently determined by choice of current ethical theories. The normative thesis, hence, puts forward a claim regarding the impartial reporting of the current set of first-principles – and not regarding the aptitude to apply those principles.

In particular, it states that not even a flawlessly smart viewer could properly gauge certain ethical matters merely by recourse to current first-principles since those ideologies do not completely cover those acts. Third, a person might contend that certain kinds of perceptions valuable in other parts of applied ethics are of partial value in the setting of computer ethics.

4.2.4. The Epistemological Thesis

The digital technologies put forward the kind of ethical issues that keep those analogies away that make it easy for the people to see the manner in which the theories concerning ethics and its primary principles, have an application in the other fields that concern the subject of applied ethics. The epistemological thesis, then, asserts no more than that the techniques that frequently help us in seeing how existing normative materials apply to specific problems are inadequate to help us with problems in computer ethics.

4.2.5. The Property Thesis

The digital technologies do have in themselves some properties that are morally correct and are different from the other artifacts that are non-living in nature, though it might happen that some living things pose such properties. Hence, one might put forward their point of view that computers have certain uniqueness and are different from other machines, in a way that it possesses certain moral values and properties.

4.2.6. Evaluating the Uniqueness Thesis

The theory which apprehends meta-ethical hurdles may be ignored and not be given a lot of importance as there is no reason to justify the points put forward in the thesis that indicate towards the limitations of existing ethical methods, which can only be possible when there are ethical methods in excess of one or there exist more ethical methods than the known three, that is, permissibility, goodness, and supererogatory.

There is no person who has come up with an argument that is in favor of any of the positions. Additionally, it is not even understood, that in what way a person could make a firm statement that supports this subject. To create a subject for a different kind of category, a person may put up a point that either one or both of these things are more in quality in a way that it has accidentally been used in the activities in which no other concept is useful.

The issue with the normative thesis's assertion that current models provide incorrect responses is that there seems to be no way to mince that impression in any current system. It is not plenty to just state that deontological theories, utilitarian theories, care theories, rights-based theories, all provide the incorrect outcome; one must validate this statement by reference to some rationally believable concept or code.

The property theory also faces problems. While supporters of this theory typically have faith in that computers possess ethical standing (i.e., are allocated an ethical responsibility of esteem), none of the unique assets of computers have any noticeable ethical significance with respect to the subject of ethical standing since these assets seem to have only instrumental value (i.e., value as a means to an end) and lack the intrinsic value (i.e., value as an end-in-itself) thought to be worthy of ethical admiration or accountability.

4.3. COMPUTER ETHICS AS A SUB-AREA IN APPLIED ETHICS

The thought that a majorly considerable kind of problems exist that incorporate some diverse properties of digital technologies, which are different and significant appears so obvious that is becomes difficult to think how it is possible that the idea could be rejected.

It is obvious that the problems regarding the intellectual property, that have been problematic due to some technologies that focus on P2P file sharing, come up due to the unique capability of the digital technology that enables itself to create and supply same form of digital music again and again and that too costing the user extremely less than the original production costs. Likewise, the ethical issues concerning free speech on the digital platforms rise because cyber skills are exclusive in making conceivable the extensive distribution of scripts and illustration files.

It can, of course, be very problematic to govern what is accurately precise response to a specific issue; hence, current groups and concepts are epistemically unknown in those cases.

But such indeterminacy, as the people have seen, is not exclusive to any specific section of ethical difficulties. Indeed, the explanation for treating remedial morals as a different field depend on various relatively ordinary deliberations.

- First, the problems in medical ethics are problems that are faced by a particular class of professionals – namely, those who work in the health care industry.
- Second, these issues have an ethically significant impact on human well-being; whether or not euthanasia, cloning, or genetic testing is morally justified can make a tremendous difference in the quality of the lives.
- Third, it may be reasonable to suppose, that took a genuine thing, that the individuals who have specialty in the issues that are in some explainable way, related to each other, are as a matter of fact, most probable to result in better quality of work. The days when it used to be comparably easier to write about issues without indulging in some proper specialization are gone away.

Yet, the very same sorts of contemplations apply to IE.

- First, the issues in digital ethics present situations for a specific class of experts – to be specific those attempting to configure, create, and actualize digital advancements.

- Second, the issues that emerge from these exercises bear imperatively on human prosperity and personal satisfaction; it is important immensely to an individual, for instance, what kind of property rights the general population have in the memories of their hard drive and in the kind of the thoughts.
- Third, it is sensible to feel that individuals who obtain a wide-extending information of the specialized attributes and moral issues of such innovations are, as an experimental issue, impressively bound to deliver quality ethical contentions tending to those issues.

4.4. GENERAL THEORIES OF INFORMATION ETHICS

There have, likewise, been a huge variety of substantive hypothetical cases about the nature and system of data ethics. A portion of these hypotheses are restricted to portraying the idea of taking care of issues in data ethics and its relationship to taking care of issues in different zones. Others endeavor to verbalize approaches or substantive rules that ought to be utilized in taking care of issues in data ethics.

However, others accept data ethics as a beginning stage for building up a more extensive procedure for tending to issues in connected ethics. A concise synopsis of a portion of these perspectives pursues underneath. Bernard Gert (1999) has contended that issues in connected ethics, incorporating issues in data ethics, ought to be settled by alluding to the "basic ethical quality."

The normal ethical quality, as Gert characterizes it, is "the [shared] moral framework that individuals use in choosing acceptable behavior while going up against good issues and in making their ethical decisions" (Gert, 1999, p. 58). As Gert calls attention to, there is substantially more assentation among people in some random culture on good issues than there is difference; however, it is very normal to concentrate vitally on what the general population differ on, "such disputable issues frame just a little piece of those issues about which individuals settle on good choices and decisions" (Gert, 1999, p.57). Issues in data ethics (and, so far as that is concerned, different zones), on Gert's view, ought to be settled by plan of action to these common good decisions. Luciano Floridi (2002) endeavors to ground a brought together way to deal with taking care of issues in data ethics in four fundamental moral rules that administer the conduct of specialists in the "infosphere;" as he portrays the issue.

By proposing that data items may require admiration regardless of whether they don't showcase human or natural properties, IE gives a general edge to moral assessment, not a rundown of edicts or point-by-point solutions (compare this with the "void" of deontological approaches). In Floridi (1999, 2001a, b, p. 298) this casing has been worked as far as moral stewardship of the data condition, the infosphere. Floridi sets four "all-inclusive laws against data entropy":

- Data entropy should not to be caused in the infosphere;
- Data entropy should be counteracted in the infosphere;
- Data entropy should be removed from the infosphere; and
- The infosphere should be ensured, broadened, enhanced, improved, and upgraded.

Jeroen van cave Hoven (1997) contends that issues in data ethics are legitimately tended to by the strategy for intelligent balance created and made celebrated by John Rawls. Moral thinking, on this view, ought to endeavor towards creating the most cognizant arrangement of convictions in which general moral cases (e.g., purposefully causing damage isn't right) and increasingly explicit case-based decisions (e.g., hitting Ken Himma in the face since his perspectives makes one distraught isn't right) help to help, legitimize, and clarify each other.

Defending a situation on an issue in data ethics will, in this manner, require demonstrating that the position has a place with the most cognizant arrangement of moral convictions. Some data ethicists have concentrated fundamentally on worries about inclinations that are verifiable in ICT or in data ethics hypothesizing.

Philip Brey (2001), for instance, contends that moral estimating ought to be a multi-disciplinary and staggered request that, in addition to other things, recognizes, and uncovers "installed normativity" in ICT. Allison Adam (2001) contends that much estimating in data ethics has neglected to consider critical issues in regards to sex and sex and backers the selection of a women's activist ethic of consideration as a method for accomplishing an alternate point of view on different issues in data ethics. Different people who are worried about the ethics in the data business have focused on telling about the extent of the field of data ethics and contrasting them with alternate fields that respect ethics somehow or another or the other. Krystna Gorniak-Kocikowska (1996) contends that the progressive overall effect of DIGITALs focuses to a requirement for another "worldwide" hypothesis of ethics.

Gorniak-Kocikowska contends that similarly as Bentham's utilitarianism was produced because of the advancement of new ICTs (i.e., the printing press), so too another moral hypothesis is probably going to rise in light of the advancement of the cutting-edge DIGITAL and related advances.

Additionally, this moral hypothesis is probably going to have a worldwide effect, in contrast to utilitarianism's constrained impact in Europe and the USA, and will supplant the moral conventions in many countries. Deborah G. Johnson (1999) has contended that DIGITAL and data ethics will, in some sense, vanish into an increasingly broad territory of moral request.

On Johnson's view, data advancements will turn out to be so completely incorporated into the lives that the general population will never again see its essence as uncommon or as one requiring a compartmentalized state of mind. Data innovations and the related issues will turn out to be completely assimilated and consolidated into the everyday lives. At the point when this occurs, the requirement for an unmistakable DIGITAL and data ethics will vanish; issues in data and DIGITAL ethics will be drawn closer comprehensively nearby different issues.

4.5. THE MORAL VALUE OF INFORMATION

One may expect in a very regular way that different kind of ethical issues that come up in association with the ICTs may, in the end, to be solved, rely on more common kind of statements about the moral esteem of the information. It is quite practical to suppose that it cannot be decided whether the rights of the intellectual property exist and are legally secured by the nation without getting to the knowledge of the value of the intellectual data.

4.5.1. Moral Standing and Two Kinds of Moral Value

Hypothetically before any substantive good issues is an increasingly broad issue concerning what creatures or elements have "moral standing." X has moral standing if and just if,

- Some ethical operator has something like one obligation with respect to the treatment of X; and
- That obligation is owed to X.

The significance of the second point ought not to be neglected. Regardless of whether a canine needs moral standing, despite everything one has an obligation not to kick the pooch; but rather that obligation is "backhanded" in light of the fact that owed to the proprietor, and not to the puppy. Assuming, notwithstanding, one owes the pooch an obligation not to kick it, at that point that is an immediate obligation since it promptly concerns the being to whom the obligation is owed.

To have moral standing and be an ethical patient, at that point, is to be the recipient of somewhere around one direct obligation. While the idea of having moral standing is generally connected with having "inherent esteem," there are two particular faculties of the thought that consider along with good hypothesizing.

The first is worried about the kind of closures that are naturally sought after by essentially judicious specialists. In this feeling of the expression, a thing, state, or element has inherent esteem if and just if for all intents and purposes normal specialists regularly esteem it as an end-in-itself; a thing has simply instrumental esteem, interestingly, if, and just in the event that it conducts as a way to some operator's end.

Factory, for instance, broadly contends that the main thing that individuals distinctively seek after for the good of its own and not for something unique is bliss. In like manner, every other thing, similar to cash or excursions, are instrumentally important as a way to anchoring the characteristically significant end of delight (see Mill, n.d.).

The views on the way that the basic value molds itself into the theory of morality in information have been varied. Mill assumed his utilitarianism from his point of view that all the people especially care about, which is a very basic thing, is happiness. If happiness remains the sole thing that individuals basically care about, then it maintains itself as the only ground of the moral evaluation.

Significantly more humbly, it is sensible to feel that individuals have a type of ethically ensured enthusiasm for what they distinctively esteem inherently – however, this reveals to us nothing about the quality or nature of such an intrigue (e.g., it reveals to us nothing about whether it ascends to the dimension of a right). The second feeling of the expression "natural esteem" is worried to distinguish a class of items that are qualified for some proportion of good regard. Elements that have characteristic incentive in this sense are moral patients meriting in any event negligible regard from for all intents and purposes levelheaded good operators.

Not at all like a substance that has just instrumental esteem, an element with inborn esteem, may not be treated as only an item to be "utilized." While the proper way to choose how to treat things with just instrumental esteem is money saving advantage investigation, things with characteristic esteem are qualified for some dimension of good thought in consultations by good operators about what to do.

Things with inborn incentive in this second sense consider moral patients with privileges that must be fulfilled. Scholars have thought about the issue of whether data or data objects have natural incentive in both of these regards.

4.5.2 "Data Objects" as Having Moral Standing

Luciano Floridi (2002) grounds his origination of IE as a general moral hypothesis in a broad case about good standing. On Floridi's view, each substance known to man can be comprehended just like a "data object" that is characteristically important and thus meriting in any event negligible good regard.

Each current element, regardless of whether aware or non-conscious, living or non-living, normal or counterfeit, has some insignificant good worth, as he places it, in excellence of its reality "qua data object." Floridi offers a few contentions for this view.

To start with, Floridi contends that the unmistakable verifiable pattern is agreeable to growing the arrangement of articles having moral standing. While the case that just individuals have moral standing has prevailed since the beginning, the Twentieth Century has seen contentions in help of the case that non-human creatures, plants, biological communities, and even workmanship objects have moral standing and are owed obligations of regard.

It is very normal, on Floridi's view, to additionally extend the class of articles with good remaining to incorporate data objects. Second, he contends that the general population can't clarify certain demonstrations without expecting that all articles merit regard in ethicalness of being data objects. Indeed, even subsequent to neglecting to have the power that is normally considered to give a help to the ethical standing, it is emphatically fought that a few people who are not proactive with their reasoning, merit some measure of regard, however, lesser than the sum they ought to have been given had they been brought into the world with increasingly dynamic personalities.

Even after failing to have the intensity that is usually taken in account to give a support to the moral standing, it is strongly contended that some individuals who are not proactive with their thinking, deserve some amount of respect, though, lesser than the amount they should have been given had they been born with more active minds.

On the off chance that the general population understand the contention as referring to the historical backdrop of such estimating as a purpose behind us to grow the ethical network to incorporate data objects, it is dangerous in light of the fact that the minor truth that scholars have, as an observational matter of chronicled certainty, extended the ethical network to incorporate creatures, plants, and land does not give us any reason, without anyone else's input, to feel that scholars should additionally grow the ethical network to incorporate data objects. Absolutely elucidating certainties about the conduct of scholars have no standardizing suggestions at all as for what the hypotheses should be.

Second, the case that Mary has moral remaining in goodness of being a data object essentially can't sufficiently clarify the sort of things that the general population do keeping in mind Mary's carcass. A stillborn youngster, for instance, is treated with unmistakably more respect than a prematurely delivered hatchling; however, both are absolutely on a similar dimension qua data objects.

Qua data objects, they comprise of a lot of suggestions that portray their different properties, activities, and capacities. Mary's inclination qua data object, at that point, can't clarify why the general population indicates more regard for her in the event that she was deceased than if she were lost. To be sure, Floridi's hypothesis comes up short on even adequate assets to clarify the distinctive dimensions of regarding the general population show to a stillborn tyke and a stone.

From the stance of the case that a thing has moral remaining in temperance of its tendency qua data object, there is no contrast between Mary qua data object and a stone qua data object; to place it in generally Quinean terms, to be qua data object is to be a lot of suggestions that has a specific intelligent structure. Therefore, Floridi's methodology can't appear to clarify even the instinct that Mary's body merits more regard than a stone.

4.6. KEY TECHNOLOGY TRENDS THAT RAISE ETHICAL ISSUES

The ethical issues have been born due to the use of IT for a long time. However, the extended use of IT has been increasing the worries regarding ethics, disturbed the social things that currently exist and has resulted in making some of the laws regarding the society redundant and severely damaged.

The intensity of the digital world that has been increasing by twice as much every one and a half year has made it easier for most of the companies to utilize these digital systems for the production processes that form the most important part of manufacturing. As a result, the dependence of the several entities on such systems, and the risk of getting vulnerable to the errors it commits and the improper and bad quality of information has increased.

The regulations and legal frameworks that have existed have not been able to adjust to this over-reliance. The standards that make sure that the data systems remain accurate and have an increased reliability, have not been accepted globally by all and neither have they been enforced on them. The latest advances in the techniques for storage of information and the costs that have been coming down with great pace have been the reason for the ever-increasing databases on various people including the employees, customers, and possible consumers, which have been kept and updated by several private and public institutions.

These techniques and innovations have regularly been violating the privacy of several entities and have made it cheaper and more effective to do so. The big firms find it extremely inexpensive to use the storage systems encompassing terabytes of data, for storing the individual identities of people, mainly their customers.

The innovations in data analytics and its techniques that concerns a huge amount of information is another trend in technology that increases the worries regarding the ethics. This happens due to the fact that the companies and government agencies are capable of figuring out extremely private information about the people and that too in a detailed way.

With the management tools for the information that have been used for a great time now, the organizations can collect the small pieces of information about the people stored on different computers and combine them with much more ease than they could in the previous times. One can think of all the ways that they can feed the information into the system such as the purchases made through credit cards, calls from their cellphones, subscription to various sites, video rentals, purchases made through e-mails, records of bank accounts, information maintained by the local state and the federal governments including the one that is maintained by the police and surfing through various web pages. Is one combines all this and thinks upon it carefully, all this data could not only make their credit information available, but also all the day-to-day habits such as tastes, driving priorities, one's associations, one's preferences in terms of books and videos they go through, and their political inclinations?

Several thousand of the most popular Web sites allow DoubleClick (owned by Google), an Internet advertising broker, to track the activities of their visitors in exchange for revenue from advertisements based on visitor information DoubleClick gathers.

DoubleClick uses this information to create a profile of each online visitor, adding more detail to the profile as the visitor accesses an associated DoubleClick site. Over time, DoubleClick can create a detailed dossier of a person's spending and computing habits on the Web that is sold to companies to help them target their Web ads more precisely (Figure 4.2).

double click

Figure 4.2: DoubleClick by Google.

Source: https://upload.wikimedia.org/wikipedia/commons/thumb/4/4f/DoubleClick_Logo.svg/2000px-DoubleClick_Logo.svg.png

For homeland security purposes, there are several highly technical security tools which are doing a good job but are overpowered with different kinds of privacy implications. Those privacy implications are scary as they showcase every single detail of an activity that has been performed by an individual.

Therefore, advances in networking, including the Internet, are beneficial and cost-effective in accessing large quantities of data and in opening the possibility of mining large pools of data remotely using small desktop machines, permitting an invasion of privacy on a scale and with a precision heretofore unimaginable.

4.7. COMMON ETHICAL ISSUES

This section shall also examine other specific ethical issues arising from IT below (Figure 4.3):

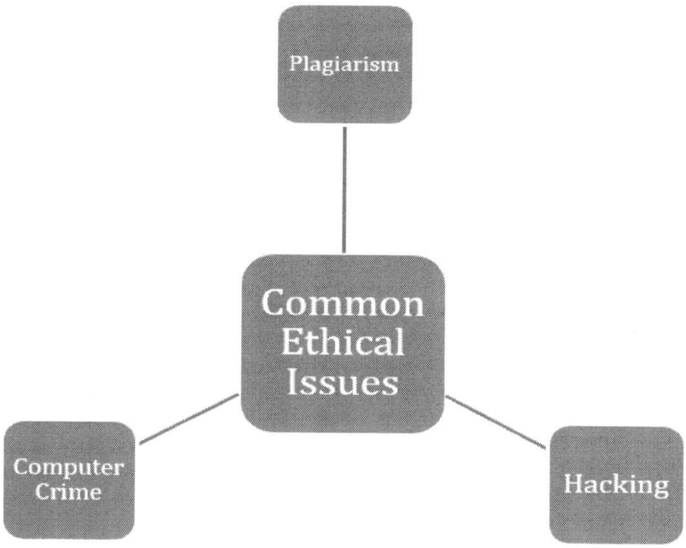

Figure 4.3: Some common ethical issues surrounding information technology.

4.8. PLAGIARISM

Plagiarism refers to a process in which someone's work is taken, without their permission, and is presented in some form claiming that the work belongs to the one who copied. This practice of plagiarism is one of the most unethical practices going around in the digital world, and nut takes place very frequently. This practice has become all the easier and more frequent as it is freely available on the internet and is accessible to all (Figure 4.4).

Figure 4.4: Say no to information plagiarism.

Source:https://cdn.pixabay.com/photo/2013/07/13/12/42/do-not-copy–160138_960_720.png

4.8.1. Information and Copyright in Education

That one sector that has gained a lot of importance in the market in the past few years due to the advancement in technology and the internet is the Commerce industry. But, in the case of education sector, the picture is not similar. There are more computers in the classroom than ever before, but there is scant evidence that they enhance the learning of basic skills in reading, writing, and arithmetic.

Having reachability to digital information is easy; it has also become apparent that most students now see libraries as antiquated institutions better used for their computer terminals than for their book collections.

Education has become easy for students who have better hands-on acquiring information in ethical as well as in an unethical manner. In a related effect, the Internet has brought plagiarism into the computer era in two distinct senses.

- Electronic texts have made students' lives easy as they can easily, "cut, copy, and paste" without giving content their own perspectives. They prepare a set of completely plagued reports which add nothing to their knowledge.

- For students, it is easy to purchase a test paper on a website, or they even get the opportunity to copy paste the assignment they have received for their internal examinations. They even commission original term papers for a fixed fee. Ironically, what the Internet gives, it also takes away.

4.8.2. Information and Copyright in Piracy

The process of copying a software in illegitimate ways is a matter of serious concern and as per the projections, about half of the programs that run on the computers of various individuals, are copies that have resulted from piracy. The programmers spend a lot of time in designing various software and programs, using a code that is finely detailed and in expanded form and hence, it needs to be secured.

Although, some of the people may put a point forward that piracy, to some extent, should be legalized as it can result in bringing up more and more people who are familiar with the knowledge of computers and digital world. But, as far as the major industries and organizations are concerned, this situation of piracy is a subject of grave concern and may cause severe damage to a company's profits and reputation.

4.8.3. Information and Copyright in File Sharing

College students have been at the leading edge of the growing awareness of the centrality of intellectual property in a digital age.

The characteristics of the recording and movie firms to not be able to avoid the sharing of file has resulted in them designing new forms and highly secured form of protection on the compact disks and digital video drives. In a certain incident that raised a lot of controversy, Sony Corporation had brought CDs to the market in 2005 that were protected against piracy. But it had a code that acted like a computer virus when inserted in the computer system. This kind of software provided a better gateway for the hackers to get into the users' computer sets and take control of their systems.

4.9. HACKING

A hacker is an individual who is knowledgeable enough to gain access without authorization to computer systems to identify security flaws. Hackers break into, or 'hack' into a system. Hacking can be undertaken for a variety of reasons, such as the wish to damage a system or the wish to understand how a system works, so that money can be made out of it (Figure 4.5).

Figure 4.5: There should be very high restrictions on the data access.

Source:https://cdn.pixabay.com/photo/2017/01/01/14/39/hacker–1944688_960_720.jpg

4.10. COMPUTER CRIME

When some of the estimates were made, about seventy-three million people for the United States had their records disclosed accidentally. Talking about one of the cases that caught attention, there happened a theft at the house of a professional at the U.S. Department of Veteran Affairs, in which a computer was stolen that had in store, data of about twenty-six million members of the U.S. military involving both – the ones who were serving and the others that had retired from the services. Though, in a consequent action, the computer was brought back, with a claim that as the thieves did not know the intensity of the machine they had taken, the data was safe.

Several illegal activities have been witnessed on computers since quite a long time which include, hacking, fraud, harassment, and embezzlement. There are also various ethical dilemmas, such as whether copying such files is as bad as stealing something.

4.11. FOUR MAIN ETHICAL ISSUES THAT EXIST IN THE MODERN WORLD

There exist a lot of challenges that are faced by the people in this world of digital advancement and interaction. These challenges generally come up from the kind of information itself. As is discussed, information is the medium that helps the minds of the individuals to expand and extend to new arenas and increases the power of the brains to achieve the desired goals, generally in a way that it gets input from the minds of others. In this way, information becomes a core and important resource that, with its intellectuality, helps the people to form their lives in a desired way and build and protect their dignity.

4.11.1. Privacy

Privacy is now something which is most commonly hacked by people through different sources. There are several questions which need to be answered before understanding the concept of privacy. Some of them are:

- What information should one be required to disclose about one's self to others?
- Under what circumstances an individual must disclose about the information without the consent of the other person?
- What information should one be able to keep strictly to one's self?

Today more than ever cautious citizens must be asking these questions.

Two kinds of situations pose a threat to the privacy of the people. The first of them is the rapid development of IT that too with an improved intensity for surveillance, correspondences, digitization, storage, and retrieval. The other one, which is a more profound form of threat, is the value of the information that has gone up in the process of taking important decisions. It is amazing how the value of information, for the people who construct policies, has gone up. These people crave for this information, even in the case that it indulges with the privacy of some other people.

Collections of information that are meant of reveal personal details of an individual have the highest potential to subside the individual from the professional as well as personal relationships. This is the ultimate cost of an invasion of privacy. So why do the people integrate databases in the first place? It is because the bringing together of disparate data makes the development of new information relationships possible.

4.11.2. Accuracy

Deception has a method for messing up individuals' lives, particularly when the gathering with the off-base data has leverage in power and expert. Consider the situation of one Louis Marches. Walks, an outsider, was a persevering man who, with his better half Eileen, at long last spared enough cash to buy a home in Los Angeles amid the 1950s.

They took out a long-haul amount in the form of loan from Crocker National Bank. Consistently Louis Marches would stroll to his nearby bank, with the loan coupon book close by, to make his installment of $196.53. He constantly checked with consideration to protected that the teller had marked "paid" in his book on the correct line, that is, only in the line of the month for which the installment was expected. What's more, he kept on doing this long after the bank had changed over to its computerized credit preparing framework.

One September a couple of years prior Marches was advised by the bank that he had neglected to make his present house installment. Walks snatched his coupon book, walked to the bank and, in broken English that indicated hints of his nation legacy, endeavored to disclose to the teller this dunning notice wasn't right. He had made his installment he guaranteed.

The stamp on his coupon book demonstrated that he had paid. The teller punched Marches' credit number on the console and surveyed the subsequent screen. Lamentably, she couldn't affirm Marches' case, nor consequently could the head teller, nor the branch administrator. At the point when looked with a PC produced screen that plainly demonstrated that his record was reprobate, this pecking order of brokers just overlooked the sections recorded in his coupon book and furthermore his chaperon raving. Befuddled, Marches left the bank in sicken.

In October, in any case, Marches obediently went to the bank to make his next installment. He was informed that he couldn't make his October installment since he was multi-month financially past due. He again demonstrated the teller his stepped coupon book. She declined to acknowledge it, and he raged out of the bank. In November he returned on calendar as he had improved the situation more than 20 years and attempted to make his installment once more, just to be informed that he was presently two months financially past due. Thus, it went until unavoidably the bank dispossessed. Eileen took in of the abandonment from an enthusiastic bank obligation gatherer while she was sleeping recouping from a heart assault.

She fallen after hearing the news and endured a close lethal stroke which incapacitated her correct side. At some point amid this scuffle Marches, who until the point that this time had done his very own lawful work, was acquainted with a lawyer who consented to guard him. They sued the bank. Eventually, following quite a while of anguish, the Marches got a settlement for $268,000. All that the bank authorities who affirmed could state was, "PCs commit errors. Banks commit errors, as well."

Today the general populations are delivering such a great amount of data about such a large number of individuals and their exercises that the presentation to issues of mistake is gigantic. What's more, this development in data likewise raises another issue: Who is responsible for all of this?

4.11.3. Property

A standout amongst the most mind-boggling issues the general population look as a general public is the topic of protected innovation rights. There are significant financial and moral concerns encompassing these rights; concerns rotating around the extraordinary qualities of data itself and the methods by which it is transmitted. Any individual thing of data can be greatly exorbitant to create in the primary occasion.

However, when it is delivered, that data has the illusive nature of being anything but difficult to imitate and to impart to other people. Additionally, this replication can happen without pulverizing the first. This makes data difficult to defend since, in contrast to unmistakable property, it ends up transferable and difficult to hold it to one's self. It is even hard to anchor proper repayments when another person utilizes individuals' data.

We as of now have a few blemished establishments that endeavor to secure licensed innovation rights. Copyrights, licenses, encryption, promises of privacy, and such outdated qualities as trust value and reliability are the most regularly utilized defenders of the protected innovation. Issue issues, be that as it may, in any case, possess large amounts of this zone. Give us a chance to concentrate on only one angle: man-made reasoning and its growing subfield, master frameworks.

To completely value the ethical predicament with respect to master frameworks it is important to keep running back the clock somewhat, around two hundred years, to the beginnings of another general public: the steam vitality mechanical society. From this vantage point, the general population may foresee a portion of the issues of the data society

No place is the potential risk to human respect so serious all things considered in the time of data innovation, particularly in the field of man-made reasoning. Professionals of man-made reasoning continue by separating information frame specialists, laborers, and the proficient, and after that embedding it into PC programming where it ends up capital in the monetary sense.

This procedure of "disemminding" learning from an individual, and accordingly "emminding" it into machines exchanges control of the property to the individuals who claim the equipment and programming. Is this trade of property justified? Consider probably the best business man-made reasoning frameworks of the day.

Who possesses, for instance, the concoction information contained in DYNDREL, the restorative learning contained in MYCIN, or the land information contained in PROSPECTOR. How is the giver of his insight to be redressed? These are among the issues the general population must purpose as increasingly savvy data frameworks are made.

Worry over protected innovation rights identifies with the substance of data. There are some similarly squeezing property rights issues encompassing the courses through with data passes. Transfer speed, the proportion of ability to convey data, is a rare and at last settled ware. It is a "typical." A typical resembles a vacant vessel in to which drops of water can be put uninhibitedly and effectively until the point that it fills and floods. At that point, its ability is no more. As an asset it is limited.

In what capacity will the restricted asset of transfer speed be assigned? Who will approach? This leads us to the fourth issue.

4.11.4. Access

The principal road to data is through proficiency. Proficiency, since around 1500 A.D. at the point when the Syrians previously imagined a consonant letter set, has been a necessity for full interest in the structure holding the system together. Every advancement in data taking care of, from the development of paper to the cutting-edge digital platforms, has put new requests on accomplishing proficiency. In a data society a subject must have somewhere around three things to be proficient: One must have the scholarly abilities to manage data. These are aptitude, for example, perusing, composing, thinking, and ascertaining. This is an assignment for training.

One must approach the data advancements which store, pass on and process data. This incorporates libraries, radios, TVs, phones, and progressively, PCs or terminals connected by means of systems to centralized servers. This is an issue in social-financial matters.

Finally, one must approach the data itself. This necessity comes back to the issue of property and is likewise an issue in social-financial aspects.

These necessities for education are an element of both the information level and the monetary dimension of the person. Lamentably, for some individuals on the planet today both of these dimensions are at present disintegrating.

Think about for a minute the social impacts of electronically put away databases. Before their development, huge amounts of information about productions, news occasions, monetary, and social insights, and logical discoveries have been accessible in printed, microfilm or microfiches frame at a moderately ease. For the greater part of us, access to this information has been significantly free.

We just went to the open or school library. The library, thusly, paid a couple of hundred dollars for the administration and made it accessible to whomever requested it. Today, in any case, a lot of this data is being changed over to automated databases and the expense to get to these databases can keep running in a great many dollars.

Regularly, access to databases is increased just by methods for obtaining a terminal or PC. For instance, in the event that one needs access to the New York Times Index through the Mead Corporation benefit one should initially approach a terminal and correspondence line and after that compensation extra connect and access charges so as to get the information.

This implies that the general population who wish to utilize this administration have a few things. To begin with, they realize that the database exists and how to utilize it. Second, they have obtained the imperative innovation to get to it. Furthermore, third, they can pay the charges for the information. Therefore, the instructive and monetary risk is extremely very high to play the advanced data amusement.

Numerous individuals can't or decide not to pay it and consequently are prohibited from taking an interest completely in the social issues. As a result, they move toward becoming data "drop outs" and over the long run, will turn into the cause of numerous social issues.

4.11.5. PAPA

Security, precision, property, and availability, these are the four noteworthy issues of data ethics for the data age. Max Plank's 1900 origination that vitality was discharged in little discrete bundles called "quanta" offered ascend to nuclear hypothesis as well as allowed the advancement of data innovation also. Semiconductors, transistors, incorporated circuits, photoelectric cells, vacuum cylinders, and ferrite centers are among the innovative yield of this logical hypothesis. Inquisitively, quantum hypothesis underlies the four issues also.

Plank's hypothesis, and all that tailed it have driven us to a point where the stakes encompassing society's approach plan are unfathomably high. In question with the utilization of atomic energy is simply the specific survival of humankind. On the off chance that the general population are impulsive, they will either explode the servers or sully the surroundings perpetually with atomic waste. In question with the expanded utilization of data, innovation is the nature of the lives should the youngsters, endure. In the event that the general population is imprudent, numerous individuals will endure data liquidation or devastation.

The ethical basis is clear. The general population must protect that data innovation, and the data it handles, are utilized to upgrade the poise of humankind. To accomplish these objectives, the general population must figure another implicit agreement, one that safeguards everybody the privilege to satisfy his or her own human potential.

- In the new implicit agreement, data frameworks ought not unduly attack an individual's protection to keep away from the insults that the understudies in Tallahassee endured.
- Data frameworks must be exact to stay away from the insults the Marches, and the Browns endured.
- Data frameworks ought to ensure the sacredness of protected innovation to keep away from the insults of accidental "disemmindment" of information from people.
- What's more, data frameworks ought to be open to stay away from the outrages of data proficiency and hardship.

This is a difficult request; however, it is one that the general population in the MIS people group should address. The general population must accept some accountability for the implicit agreement that rises up out of the frameworks that they plan and actualize. In outline, the general population must guarantee that the stream of those little parcels of vitality and data called quanta, which Max Plank sequestered to us somewhere in the range of 85 years before, are utilized to make the sort of world in which the general population wishes to live.

REFERENCES

1. Einar, H.K., (2007). Foundational issues in information ethics. *Library Hi-Tech*, [online] *25*(1), pp. 79–94. Available at: https://pdfs.semanticscholar.org/2257/d355376bf302055b99657b216a5efc6621a2.pdf [Accessed 15 Nov. 2018].
2. *Ethical and Social Issues in Information Systems*, (n.d.). [eBook] Available at: http://wiki.stoa.usp.br/images/0/02/MIS-cap4.pdf [Accessed 15 Nov. 2018].
3. Mason, R., (n.d.). *Four Ethical Issues of the Information Age.* [eBook] Available at: https://www.gdrc.org/info-design/4-ethics.html [Accessed 15 Nov. 2018].
4. Ugbogbo, S., & Michael, A., (2016). Ethical issues in information technology- a conceptual approach. *Igbinedion University Journal of Accounting*, [online], 2. Available at: https://www.iuokada.edu.ng/journals/5B6AA29B40ADBA7.pdf [Accessed 15 Nov. 2018].
5. Floridi, L. (2002). What is the Philosophy of Information?. Metaphilosophy, 33(1&2), pp.123-145.
6. G. Johnson, D. (1999). *Sorting Out the Uniqueness of Computer-Ethical Issues*. [ebook] Available at: https://core.ac.uk/download/pdf/41174283.pdf [Accessed 17 Mar. 2019].
7. Gorniak-Kocikowska, K. (1996). The computer revolution and the problem of global ethics. Science and Engineering Ethics, 2(2), pp.177-190.
8. A. Adam. Computer Ethics in a Different Voice. Information and Organization, 11(4): 235–61, 2001.
9. Brey, P. (2001). Disclosive computer ethics. ACM SIGCAS Computers and Society, 30(4), p.10.
10. Floridi, L. (1999). *Ethics and Information Technology*, 1(1), pp.33-52.
11. Floridi, Luciano. (2001). Information ethics: an environmental approach to the digital divide. Pp. 13 -22
12. Gert, B. (1999). Ethics and Information Technology. Ethics and Information Technology, 1(1), pp.53-60.

5

International Development and Computer Ethics

CONTENTS

Information ethics (IE) deals with the moral values and ethical standards related to the privacy, protection, and security of information. The definition and the beginning of IE as subject and the various aspects regarding IE have been discussed. The major aspects of IE are the micro ethical and macro ethical approaches that delineate the concept of IE have been elucidated. The various theoretical approaches and different perspectives like the socio-philosophical, information ecology perspective and the systems and technology perspective have been explained. The classification, factors, and different principles of IE have been discussed.

5.1. INTRODUCTION

The field of IE have been studied deeply studied over a period for a period of more than twenty years. The term IE was initially made by the Rafael Capurro, director of International Center for Information Ethics (ICIE) in the year nineteen eighty-seven.

The study of ethics is more inclined towards the moral values and its concepts. Concepts related to values could be values that could be good or bad, right or wrong. It all depends on the actions related to the groups and norms. Therefore, ethics and their studies take a deep dive into the issues that are more or less related to practical decision-making (Veatch, 1977). In the case of "Computer software systems," most of the decisions are taken after a complete analysis has been made through computer software which also comprises data/information storage and manipulation, data availability, and 'alternatives' formulation and selection.

There was a conference on IE sponsored by the Graduate School of Library and Information Science, and from then there are a lot of new schools, magazines, and various conferences started to study the field of IE.

The IE was started as a university program by the University of Pittsburgh and Kent State University. The IE is a field that is grounded on the various ethical aspects of the data process in the society and by the data obtained from the performance of different individuals, groups, and organizations.

The IE signifies a setup of different moral values and behavior rules in the context of various related factors of the information environment. The experts state that the IE is understood as the art and science that enables receptivity and approaches to perceive ethical standards that are used to obtain, process, and utilize information for the information behaviors

(Capurro, 2000; Fallis, 2010; Floridi, 2010; Froelich, 2004; Rubin and Froelich, 2010; Sturges, 2009) (Figure 5.1).

Figure 5.1: The different aspects of ethics.

Source: https://upload.wikimedia.org/wikipedia/commons/7/7e/Business_ethics.jpg

IE is such a comprehensive topic that it also covers that discipline which involves evaluating human behavior, their values and the way they make their choices (whether they are rational or irrational) apart from following just the principles related to philosophy and ethics. IE is also related to other dimensions of information which involve internet, biology, politics, business, and ethics of information systems, media, and medicine.

In the case of IE, different kinds of studies are involved which could be normative, descriptive, general, analytical, applied or special in nature. Each professional (especially scientists) is required to oblige to fulfill its moral responsibilities, and these responsibilities are supposed to be followed by a required professional code. The main divisions of IE are:

- IE of agents;
- IE of users; and
- IE of makers.

As discussed above, few professional codes which are required to be followed by any professional are:

- Codes of ethics of IFLA, ALA, ACM;
- Regulations of ASIST and ALISE; and
- Codes of ethics of UNESCO.

To have a deeper insight into IE, several conferences have taken place in the past ten years which were mostly sponsored by UNESCO, World Summits on the Information Society equally engage in IE issues. The major concerns of IE are related to the moral responsibility of makers and users of information and of information professionals. This is so because these two roles could be easily interchange their roles and responsibilities with the help of technology. New knowledge concerning human information behavior makes it equally important now to build up a theoretical frame of IE.

As stated by Froelich in 2004, other than the roles and responsibilities, there are other dimensions related to IE, which are; ethics of information use, ethics of information systems and technologies, and ethics of information society and information strategies. Based on these dimensions several researchers believe that information is that discipline which helps in creating a well-structured framework for interconnectedness of different value aspects of work with information.

It is IE that help in understanding the importance of moral values and also their criticality. Moral values here are referred to the information that is used by an individual for any purpose. IE is beneficial in evaluating and interpreting ethical issues related to information. The study of the survey of approaches to theories and practical uses of IE in information science, with a view of the contexts of human information behavior and information ecology.

The analysis regarding the socio-philosophical approaches and the methods regarding the different systems and technology is needed to be understood. Therefore, the different novel aspects of classification of IE according to the different factors and value analysis that are explained below. The focus is on the theoretic and practical research to study the novel models that assist in the development of the surroundings with the IE.

First, few implications of ethics of adopting a specific approach to designing of system are analyzed. Next, the significant issues of ethics described are in turn presented. The chapter concludes with the description of professional codes of ethics, as well as a basis for having an ethical approach to system designing and development.

Cyberethics are mainly concerned with the ethical issues that are related to the cyberspace or internet. Topics in this field comprises artificial intelligence (AI), expert systems and the capability of robots.

5.2. DEFINING THE FRAMEWORK OF INFORMATION ETHICS

5.2.1. Definition

IE is defined as the ethics of several fields that produce data and generate information along with distribution of knowledge. These fields are library and information science, education, technologies, censorship, privacy, research reviewing and others. This definition of IE was given by Robert Hauptmann, who is the editor of the Journal of IE magazine that is being published from the year 1992.

5.2.2. Important Aspects of Information Ethics

There are two important features that need to be considered when defining the IE and they are:

- Information; and
- Ethics.

Information refers to the information behavior, information system, and general information in various contexts. Ethics refers to the moral and ethical values that are related to the information. However, there is need to understand the specifications of the framework of both aspects so that they help in regulating the way these affect the content and concretization of the actual life examples.

To acquire a universal approach towards IE in one required frame, theories related to information science should be acknowledged properly, and researchers should also look into the way these theories have represented information. One way to tackle this is by identifying the different levels of interaction between ethics and information (individual, group, organizational, societal).

The information is defined as a framework which brings together cognitive, biological, social, physical, and technological components of information environment when an individual aspires to gain meaning out of something. Information is constructed socially in concrete, real-life instances of information behavior.

Each information has its own context, and the context is a circumstance or a situation which gets created and has a meaning to that one or relatable situation or an event. Since context is dynamic, it is contingent on personal characteristics, social circumstances and information space.

There are two different approaches that are used to define IE. These methods are:

- Microethical; and
- Macroethical.

Various researchers differentiate between morals as ethics applied in praxis, and morals as a moral practice. There is a distinction between theoretical reflection on the one hand, and concrete information behavior and information systems on the other.

However, there is need to use an interdisciplinary approach with the merger of different branches like the information science, philosophy, new media studies, as the subject is too complex to understand by just studying a single field.

5.2.3. Microethical Approach

As per the definition stated by Microethics, IE is an indispensable part of human information behavior, and wherein there are several factors and contexts related to IE which are represented by information behavior.

Microethics defines the IE as a process with several stages of human activity of utilization of information that is categorized by the human adaptation to information environment. The factors that regulate IE are the human being, the different sources of data and the various products that have been made by utilizing information and producing information.

With the help of a context, it becomes easy to summarize the ownership of information, authorized use of information, and information activities within the information environment.

5.2.4. Macroethical Approach

The Macroethical approach is more inclined towards the application of norms of ethical nature. This helps in digging into that information that are based on societal and global levels. At a global level, IE takes the shape of information ecology. The macroethical framework deals with the issues that are related to information society, particularly its digital divide, environmental ethics (man as part of information environment), and the ecological approach to the life cycle of information.

It is a social framework for the moral values of information use and the interconnectedness of the social with the technological. Common discourse that probes information existence is formulated here, and issues of coexistence of information objects and man in the information environment are examined.

The microethical and macroethical approach enable in defining the field of IE as an idea based on the information behavior. IE is a kind of information behavior of the creators, users, and information experts where there is a value system that is based on the choice making and problem-solving in the field of utilization of information.

5.3. THEORETICAL APPROACHES OF INFORMATION ETHICS

IE is examined both at the level of theory and at the level of applied IE. In approaches to information science of the last twenty years, information science is dominated by the concepts of intellectual freedom, freedom of speech and press, and free access to information (particularly in electronic environment). The theoretical approach of information science enables to differentiate among the socio-philosophical and system-based approaches of IE.

5.3.1. Socio-Philosophical Perspective on Information Ethics

The socio-philosophical perspective of IE denotes that the study of general ethics. The different socio-philosophical classes of information science are epistemology, ontology, and ethics. In Ancient Greek tragedy, "parrhesia "means freedom of speech and personal devotion to truth. This concept has recently been incorporated into research concerning IE and the ethical use of information.

There are several novel understandings in the network-based electronic environments which state that different new types of information behavior are exhibited and generated when the new media is being utilized Capurro (2005).

There is an idea from the history which projects ethics as a philosophical domain that would generate different theoretical concepts. Teleological perspective links ethics with that which is useful, makes sense, serves order, and has a goal.

Theological perspective represents normative ethics, deontological perspective emphasizes a basic moral imperative (ensuing from reason—Kant's categorical imperative), axiological perspective is based on value preference (N. Hartman), rationalistic perspective refers to societal consensus for the solution of practical conflicts, while utilitarian perspective, represented by the philosophy of J. Mill, emphasizes ethical values related to achieving happiness and pragmatism.

The understanding of IE is dependent on the several cultures and the cultural differences that play a role in formation of information society. For example, there are a lot of differences in the ethical and moral values of the western cultures which are based on the fundamentals of Christianity and eastern cultures that are based on Buddhism, Hinduism, and Islam.

There is focus on the value of IE in the western tradition with respect to the framing of power and concepts of accessibility, reliability of information and the extensive of the data. (Capurro, 2005).

The key is the use of information as part of intellectual freedom and truth-seeking. This has to do with norms of information behavior when information and information technologies are used to communicate information. Western approach, in theory, refers to universal rationalistic (often Christian) values that apply to information use. Eastern (philosophical) approaches remove a universal representation of values, preferring instead to moral values that reflect man as a part of his environment.

Luciano Floridi (2010) introduces a conception of IE related to his philosophy of information. He argues that IE is a part of environmental ethics. Information technologies and information systems are also incorporated into the environment via value systems.

There are three main elements that are part of IE according to Floridi. They are:

- Information as resource;
- Information as product; and
- Information as target.

Social agents set these relationships into motion in information environment. The ontological conception of L. Floridi ascribes information value to each object in the information environment. It is the objective of ecological control of the information environment to cultivate information objects and make them prosper with information science tools (systems, products, services, organization of information) in the information environment.

There is major role played by the values that have been obtained from empirical research that involves academic information that is extracted from technologies, resources, community, and communication that offers significant support to the creativity of the people.

The IE is defined as a fragment of information ecology which is a combination of ideologies, morals, and guidelines of usage of information products of separate representatives in the data atmosphere.

The analysis of relevance has evidenced predominance of value of trust of experts (cognitive authority) as the basis for further models of relevance in an electronic environment.

5.3.2. RPT Model (Resource, Target, and Product Model Resource, Target, and Product Model)

This gives rise to a model called as the RPT model (Resource, target, and product model)

- **Information as resource:** The use of information in IE where information is valuable resource.
- **Information as product:** The generation of information by IE is the use of information as a product.
- **Information as target:** The environment of information is affected by the IE.

Ethics of information as a resource: Ethics of information as a resource can be described as those moral values which are incorporated when there is a presence or absence of information resources in a secured form. Moral values concern accessibility, safety, reliability, and exactness of information resources. The focus lies on safeguarding the anonymity, supporting a fair treatment towards an information and its resource and evaluating the disinterested evaluation.

Ethics of information as a product: Ethics of information as a product can be described as a social agent which act as a producer of an information. The production lies within the restrictions and possibilities of the information environment. Responsibility concerning creation is the most important value, as is compliance with rules (legislative), or issues such as plagiarism, propaganda, advertisement, and misinformation.

Ethics of information as target: Ethics of information as target is related to the impact that is made after the moral judgment on the information environment. An example for the same could be; Disturbing the information environment intentionally which would also comprise activities which would be unethical or unacceptable such as "hacking" (unauthorized access to information systems), infringement of privacy, and piracy on the one hand, and securing of private ownership freedom of speech, censorship, filtering, and content control on the other.

5.3.3. Information Ecology Perspective of Information Ethics

According to Floridi in 2010, "The ecological approach to IE perceives information both as a method and an entity of environment and the world." If any object of the information environment may be considered an information object, it may also be taken into consideration a global view of the entire life cycle of information belonging to ecological IE.

There is an ontological approach that has been made by Capurro and Floridi about the concept of IE. There are two concepts proposed by them, and they are:

- Environmental Approach proposed by Floridi; and
- Digital ontology proposed by Capurro.

These two models differ in the fundamental concepts which formed the basis for this classification.

Environmental Approach: The view of IE as an environmental model which states that there is connection between the value obtained from the information of an object to the existence of the object. There is a need for the objects of information to grow; hence, the contamination of the infosphere is the major component of the IE.

However, the environmental model proposed by Floridi does not concentrate on the social concerns of IE which is a major drawback.

Digital Ontology: The IE of a digital objects with respect to their interaction with the surrounding environment and their respective social, intercultural, and moral values is called as Digital Ontology. The IE is related to the principles of ecological, political, economic, and cultural domains (Capurro, 2005).

Therefore, it is necessary that IE should be applicable to those issues that are intercultural in nature with respect to the digital divide. They could also be applicable in a scenario where a change in behavior is witnessed and a situation where moral values of life become affected by developmental changes of the infosphere and internet.

5.3.4. Information Ethics from the Point of View of Systems and Technology

There are a lot of concepts connected to the IE of the information society that have risen from the related areas like digital and computer ethics. Broad availability of information in digital forms has generated many concrete issues concerning ownership of digital records and digital information.

The various aspects related to IE are categorized into different types (Zwass, 2010). They are:

- Privacy;
- Accuracy;
- Property;
- Access.

These are the fundamental concepts that are used in the design, expansion, and utilization of information systems.

The right of the people to secure the information about their personal lives from unlicensed access is called as privacy. Privacy is considered by different scientists of IE as a basic aspect of social science (Cibangu, 2012).

The issues related to the regulation of clicks are generally connected to the misuse of information with an intent to do marketing. For an instance, the ACM code of ethical conduct is known to make experts to value privacy as a fundamental rule, and many industries are reviewing these issues as an aspect if self-regulation. The correct and accurate data is connected to the collecting of information of high standards and maintain privacy and security of information systems. The accurate information must to totally mistake free with all the relevant content with comprehensive information.

The right of possession of information must generally be obtained by following the law. Therefore, intellectual property is an integral component of ethics as it deals with irrelevant possession of creative content by a person or an organization. The expansion of internet services, however, has forged an inviting environment for infringement of this right.

The major doubt is that to what extent are the digital products are owned by an individual. There is need for latest modifications and updated law and ethics to make decisions about the digital products and information.

There are various variations that are present at a personal, national, and international level with respect to the retrieval of information.

There is overlay of information between computer ethics and IE with the major variation being that the focus of computer ethics is on the quality of information related to system designing, management of system security, integrity, and correction of data and the focus of IE is on the securing of information and maintaining privacy of data (Froehlich, 2004). Some ethical dilemmas are embedded in issues regarding *who the owner of the data is, how their use can be regulated, and how to build trust in digital services*.

There are lot of synopses of codes of conducts which are called as etiquette that are available across the internet which consists of rules of respect, privacy, and ownership rights to misuse of power, regulate the sharing of improper data, and publication of one's own work without using others work.

5.4. ETHICAL APPROACHES TO SYSTEM DESIGN

Even at the broadest of the levels, the ethics can get implemented or applied, in accordance with the entire approach, to the structure of the provided system. Nevertheless, such approach might tend to differ dramatically in terms of their respective potentiality so that they could be able to cope with the issues related to morality or ethics.

Varied conventional approaches towards the growth or development along with the structure of the systems, for instance: the process of analyzing or assessing the systems that has been designed along with the various other structured procedures or SSADM, which is also known as the most known procedure for the development in various countries possessing major concentration on the issues that are technical in nature in comparison to the issues belonging to the human beings.

It generally tends to consider various facets of technology belonging to the development or the growth of the pertaining system by the process of segregating the development of the system within minor tasks. It possesses the involvement of the varied characterization of the levels or the stages for example: assessment or the analysis of the needs, provided specification of the requirements, alternatives for the technical systems, design or the structure of physics, feasibility, varied substitutes for the business systems along with the logical designs.

All of the provided levels generally tend to have an inclusion of the enumeration of the provided steps as well as all of those steps, thus, involves certain enumeration of the tasks, which are required to be performed.

At the bottom level, SSADM includes around 230 tasks. Amongst the 230 tasks, not all are executed in a specific implementation. The stage definition informs the developer regarding the preceding products that are fed into the next stage and what are the products that will be created by the particular stage.

SSADM tends to put an effort in describing three perspective regarding the pertaining system as to how all the items of the data present within the system, would be able to sweep away from it, how the provided items of the data are interrelated with one another, how all of the items within the data tend to transit over the time period (Kendall and Kendall, 1999).

Whereas the pertaining 230 tasks, which have been composing the SSADM in the recent times does not tend to particularly possess a concern over the issues related to the ethics or morality, it can be apprehended that the various steps or the stages or the provided tasks belonging to SSADM that possess the potentiality of getting restructured so that they could assist them in doing likewise.

The substitute approach for this is the model of CATWOE, which helps in identifying or recognizing the various customers, processes of conversion, the respective environment, view or the perception of the world, actors along with the owners.

As it clearly comprises different roles of people, it can support the ethical concerns mainly if augmented by the building of an ethical conflict web (Wood-Harper et al., 1996).

The provided approach, then, tries to have an identification or the recognition of who all are doing what and for whom are they are doing it, to whom all are they accountable, what all expectations or the assumptions have been made related to it, as well as within what environment this process is occurring.

Limitations related to the approach of CATWOE are not at all similar to that of the approach related to SSADM, as it never provides with the information as to how one should be building a specific system. In addition to it, it generally tends to make assumption regarding the varied workers along with the managers that they usually discuss their respective issues in open.

The basic notion belonging to the ecologies of the pertaining information (Davenport and Prusak, 1997) has been considered as a novel approach in accordance with the development of the provided system, which considers the technology in terms of the notion of the various individuals, practices along with the institutes or the organization, which is being related to the utilization of the system.

This approach is based on analogies with ecology such as information diversity (species diversity), information environment evolution (biological evolution), emphasis on observation and description, and a focus on people and information behavior. The emphasis on people and the method by which they utilize the information must be an enhancement over the conventional approaches; however, it lacks the particular emphasis on the ethics described by Wood Harper et al. (1996).

But, in accordance with any of the procedure related to the structure of the systems, wherein there is an obligation that there should not be much of concentration on the ways as to how all the pertaining individuals tend to make utilization of the provided information, but also on the manner in the present people tend to utilize the systems or the provided information in a wrong manner, and thus, clearly or tacitly providing with an indication regarding the ways of utilizing the systems and how they shouldn't be.

Quality of life: Various systems belonging to the computer have usually been projected to have an improvement or enhancement within their respective workplace, but also within the personal lives of the pertaining individuals. Nevertheless, the present systems might in real, be deteriorating the basic quality of the life of people who are working, with the help of:

- Increasing fatigue, stress, boredom, and depersonalization;
- Deskilling the workforce. It declines the responsibility, control as well as job satisfaction;
- Safety as well as health concerns like headaches, eyestrain, and repetitive strain injury (Forester and Morrison, 1994).

Various personal computers have led to certain transitions within the procedures related to the work. The key transition that occurred rose from the greater level of accessibility belonging to the packages of the statistical software that tends to present the basic sophisticated power of the analysis within pertaining hands of the various people along with the lesser knowledge regarding statistics. The prevalent use of the systems of word processing has consequence in the authors of documents, which is accountable to produce final copies instead of typing them by the secretarial staff.

Particularly, a system should not enhance the damage to the least privileged or risk enhancing damage in already damaged environments.

This is surely being considered as an aspiring test of the morality as well as ethics for the provided software, being presented with the required intellectual, financial, social, economic as well as political reach, which all the existing software have the capability to possess, wherein this specific perception holds the restrictions grounded on the various operations, for instance: how distant or in what all manner, they are being required to have an extensions within the penumbra in order to have an inclusion of all the parties, which have been severely affected.

5.5. COMPUTER ETHICS AS A REFERENCE DISCOURSE OF INFORMATION SYSTEMS

The basic argument being related with the ethics of the information as well as the communication technology is entirely dependent on the identification of the ethics or the morality belonging to the computers that can certainly be viewed, as the generic dissertation for the research of IS that is being somehow related with the morality or the ethics.

Thus, in order to have a determination of this, the individual is required to provide an evidence that all the theories, approaches along with the topics belonging to the ethics of the computer have been replicated with the help of IS. It is significant to consider that this relationship is not a kind of one way and one can easily observe an opposite relationship with IS as a discourse of reference for computer ethics.

As a reference discourse, the role of computer ethics for ethics-related IS research develops as a much more protruding form when a person looks at the themes being explored.

In here, privacy has been considered as the most prevailing matter related to the ethics belonging to the information as well as the communication technology, which tends to play a greater part within the research of IS and thus, is being wholly related with the ethics or morality. In here, not just, it is being considered as the first and the foremost P within PAPA acronym belonging to the Mason; it is also a theme of recurring in various protruding ethics related IS researches. The challenging relationship between security and privacy also invents its reflection in the IS research.

Simultaneously, there is a lot of emphasis on the ethical context of the application of computing technologies in IS. Nevertheless, one can argue that there is a substantial overlap in the themes of interest between computer ethics and ethics-related IS research.

Thus, in order to provide with the summarization of this, one might present with the opinion that the ethics belonging to the computers tend to play an essential part of the dissertation of the various references for the research of the IS being related with the ethics or morality in the way that most of the important tracts of their respective interest can be discovered within both of them. This does not really make a robust statement regarding the way of the relationship between the two.

A further possibility would be to see both streams of research reflect the public interest in important social concerns. For the purposes of this paper, the details of the mechanisms facilitating it are of secondary importance.

Although the ground for this turn was prepared by those working in computer ethics, it is worth emphasizing the new discourse and its advantages in comparison to (traditional) computer ethics. This point is made in detail in the following section, which introduces the concept of RRI in ICT as the next step in building on computer ethics.

5.6. TAXONOMY OF INFORMATION ETHICS

There are mainly four classes of IE theory according to Don Fallis (2007). They are as follows (Figure 5.2):

- Theories based on the consequence;
- Theories based on the ethics;
- Theories based on the duty and theories based on the law; and
- Theories based on the virtue.

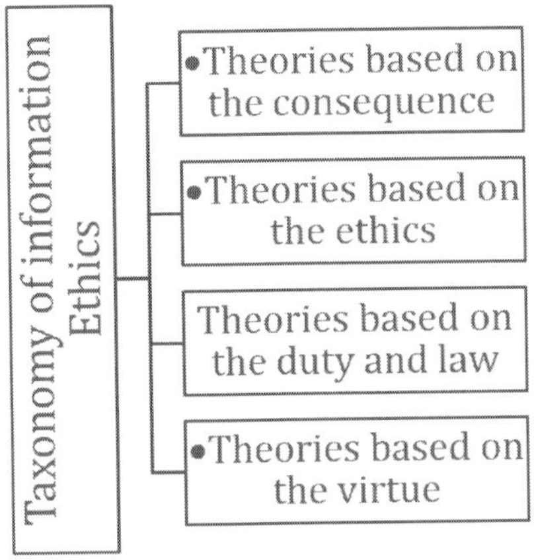

Figure 5.2: The taxonomy of information ethics.

There are several issues related to IE which are conceptual in nature. IE may be determined on methodology levels of cognitivism, within which IE forms a part of cognitive and constructive development of the mind, and of socio-cognitive approach dominated by ethical building of concepts in shared information spaces, such as concepts from science disciplines.

This understanding and analysis of different concepts of IE is represented in the following table.

Table 5.1: Taxonomy of Concepts of Information Ethics in Information Process

Obtaining information	Access to information, selection, codes, verification of correctness of information, prediction of consequences, information needs— contexts: task, issue, digital divide, information scarcity
Use of information	Accessibility, free access to information, intellectual freedom, censorship, copyright, legal use, commercial use
Organization of knowledge	Exactness of information, structures of knowledge, reliability, quality of information, filtering
Social networks	Community, protection, power structures, power, responsibility, manipulation, communication
Information sharing	Privacy, collective wisdom, management of knowledge, freedom of speech, confidentiality, data protection

Generation of information	Ownership, responsibility, rules, intellectual freedom, plagiarism, copyright, principle of least effort, morality
Online interaction	Security, protection, authenticity verification, antisocial behavior: piracy, cybercrime: flaming, trolling, spamming

The ethical issues surface with the duties as well as restrictions on the use and creativity of information (citation ethics, responsibility, reliability, availability, security, exactness of information privacy) and information rights (information literacy, intellectual freedom).

5.7. GLOBALIZATION AND COMPUTER ETHICS

Today, computer ethics is progressively evolving into a wider and also more significant field that might practically be known as "global IE." The international networks such as the Internet and mainly the world-wide-web are linking the people all around the world.

Krystyna Gorniak-Kocikowska in her paper, "The Computer Revolution and the Problem of Global Ethics," for the first time in history that, "efforts to develop mutually agreed standards of conduct, and efforts to advance and defend human values, are being made in a truly global context."

So, for the first time in the history of the earth, ethics, and values will be debated and transformed in a context that is not limited to a geographic region, or constrained by a specific religion or culture. This may very well be one of the most important social developments in history. Consider just a few of the global issues:

Global Laws: If the users of computers in the US wants to secure their freedom of speech on the internet. Around two hundred countries are interconnected by the internet; thus the constitution of the US is just a "local law" on the web; it really does not apply to the rest of the world.

Global Cyber business: The world is quite close to have the technology that can give electronic privacy as well as security on the internet enough to conduct the transactions of international business safely. Once the technology at its right place, there will be a robust enlargement of international cyberbusiness.

Global Education: If inexpensive access to the global information network is provided to rich and poor alike -- to poverty-stricken people in ghettos, to poor nations in the "third world," etc.—for the first time in history, nearly everyone on earth will have access to daily news from a free press; to texts, artworks and documents from inordinate libraries as well as museums of the world; to religious, political, and social practices of peoples all over the place.

What will be the influence of this abrupt and deep "global education" upon isolated communities, political dictatorships, religious practices, coherent cultures, etc.? As great universities of the world begin to offer degrees and knowledge modules via the internet, will "lesser" universities be damaged or even forced out of business?

5.8. FACTORS AND VALUE PRINCIPLES OF INFORMATION ETHICS

There is a phenomenon called the ethical tension which originates from the professionals and information institutions that are at work due to the large volume of written and unwritten rules and institutionalized and individual professional principles. It can be described through an example of a corporate world where ethics play a key role in determining an individual's future in that company. This is so because it talks about the effects of an employer's ethical code, ethical codes of professional companies, customer pressure regarding provision of services, personal ethical convictions, and ethical, societal norms (Rubin and Froelich 2009).

Apart from the corporate world, ethical factors have a huge impact on the library and information studies. There are the factors of social usefulness, survival, social responsibility, and respect of man's personality.

The concept of IE is slowly becoming a part of university education in many programs of library and information science, and professional organizations, such as American library association (ALA), Association for information science and technology (ASIST) and Association for Library and Information Science Education (ALISE).

5.9. EXAMPLES OF ETHICAL DILEMMAS WHEN USING AND PROCESSING INFORMATION

The main example of IE is citation ethics. This is related particularly to ease of access and use or abuse of electronic information. Issues of plagiarism have therefore been more closely monitored in student works, while citation ethics is included in courses of information literacy.

The different instances include matters of defense of intellectual property with the help of novel methods of information utilization in digital science, which is called as "Creative Commons." A state of issue pertains due to the stress that accumulates when a situation related to the right to information and freedom of speech arises, particularly as regards censorship and filtering of information. Restrictions may apply particularly to dissemination of malignant information (These are that information which might not be suitable for the kids to go through or would be inappropriate for them to understand.).

Use of information systems and technologies is another main concern that gets originated when encountered by an individual. For example, digital divide, provision of electronic information services in governmental areas, cybernetic crime. Maximum number of solutions to ethical dilemmas is contingent on existing regulations (laws, codes) on the one hand, and on the formation of information policies and information literacy that underpin man's information behavior on the other.

The best-suited method for understanding the matters related to IE is information ecology (Capurro, 2005; Floridi, 2010). It has now become an indispensable part of interpretation of relationships between man, information, and technologies, placing emphasis on the positive values of the cultivation of information environment and services for advancement of knowledge in society.

For example, the technologies established by the companies like Volkswagen and YouTube have as well as continue to have a reflective influence on the society. For more than ten years, YouTube has formed the way people make, share, and consume the content of video. Likewise, it is quite hard to imagine a world deprived of Volkswagen cars, as since the early of 20th century, the company has been a mainstay.

There is a reason why incidents leave an impact on the society. For example, incidents like "YouTube's controversial recommended videos incident" and Volkswagen's emission scandal were few to name that had a long-lasting impact on the society and especially on the kids (a major point of concern for the parents).

The rush to meet deadlines and sell products can cause delivery teams to overlook security, unit, integration, and performance tests that eliminate problematic bugs or other issues. This is a prime example of the mindset of why, for the delivery of software, code of ethics is required in the tech companies to assure their aims are good willed while delivering the product. As one identical code of ethics like the Hippocratic Oath in the medical profession can be a resolution for the software industry, it is also important to teach delivery teams how to ask the right questions when considering the ramifications for emerging innovations. The ethics question may be different for different types of organizations as well, leaning more toward an individual, organizational view rather than a global one.

The organizations can use various values that are commitment, courage, focus, openness, and respect. They provide help to guide the decision-making and increase team dynamics (Figure 5.3).

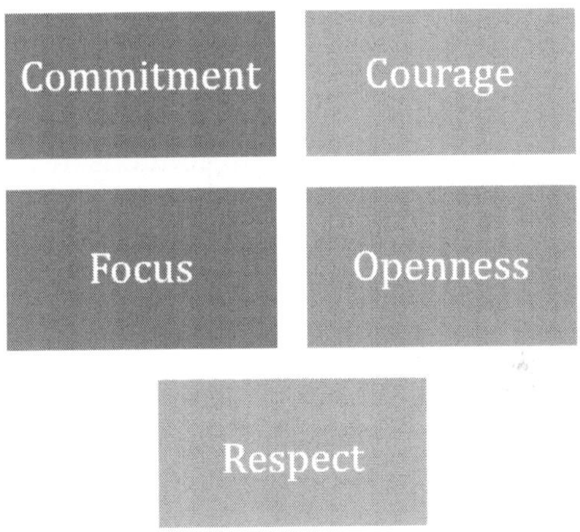

Figure 5.3: Values of an organization.

- **Commitment:** In the case of IE, commitment could be described as a form of trust an individual or a team have towards the agile approach and its values. Generally, it is believed that people working in the same team adopt similar approach towards a problem, but by making the commitment explicit as an individual, team, and organization, they all start from the same baseline. This might create a situation where one team member would not follow the information ethics.
- **Courage:** It is the courage that motivates an individual to speak up and call out unethical behavior by management that can influence work being produced. Various organizations usually believe that the bad decision will ultimately disappear if you don't say anything.

It is important to motivate people in such a way that they have transparency within the team as this would help them in achieving their respective goals ethically. It is not just the leaders' responsibility to encourage the team to follow the ethical line, but everyone must have that sense of responsibility towards the work they do and should follow an ethical line to accomplish the goal.

- **Focus:** Instead of working independently, teams are more effective when they collaborate on small sets of customer-driven outcomes. Therefore, company leaders should empower their teams to tackle the most important tasks first as they work toward a final product. Concentrating on a task at a particular point of time assures that the teams are pushing the best resources only for the production of final product any organization can be honored of.
- **Openness:** A leader must not encourage commitment and courage, but should also help the team to be open amongst the team members. This will build trust on each other and would help them take the track with complete positivity while achieving the required goal. Openness within the team helps in creating transparency and would give space and scope to everyone to develop their skills by their own, the phrase "fail fast" is often used to describe agile approaches, but actually, it is "learn fast." Openness is a prerequisite to that mantra.
- **Respect:** Above all, leaders of the company must respect the diverse backgrounds, variety of skills and experience of their team members. Giving respect to the team members and presuming they have ideal intentions can easily lead to the conversations which can be utilized to resolve the conflicts present in an organization and enhances the performance of the team. When people feel respected and know they are being heard, they can fully support company decisions, even if the decision was not their preference.

5.10. CONCLUSION

IE is a big challenge to maintain in the age where people are getting used to the advancements that are taking place in the technological world. The focus, however, is generally towards theoretical aspects of IE and identification of basic socio-philosophical and system- and technology-based approaches to and taxonomies of IE. The main challenges of researchers are more inclined towards the development of theories of information behavior and information theories.

With regard to the near future, issues of importance are regulations concerning intellectual property, ownership, plagiarism, negative phenomena and spam dissemination on the one hand, and issues of securing equality of access, such as digital divide, and censorship, on the other.

The latest replicas of IE are known to upsurge receptivity of social and ethical standards of information behavior and information practice, that enable to discover the right equilibrium between information privileges and responsibilities, penalties, and rules of information behavior, and approachability, frankness, and reliability of information.

REFERENCES

1. Froehlich, T., (2004). *A Brief History of Information Ethics*. [online] Bid.ub.edu. Available at: http://bid.ub.edu/13froel2.htm [Accessed 22 Nov. 2018].
2. Oldknihovna.nkp.cz., (n.d.). *Information Ethics in the Context of Information Ecology [Jela Steinerová]*. [online] Available at: http://oldknihovna.nkp.cz/knihovna141_suppl/1401024.htm [Accessed 15 Nov. 2018].
3. Stahl, B., Eden, G., Jirotka, M., & Coeckelbergh, M., (2014). From computer ethics to responsible research and innovation in ICT. *Information & Management*, [online] *51*(6), pp. 810–818. Available at: https://www.sciencedirect.com/science/article/pii/S037872061400007X [Accessed 22 Nov. 2018].
4. Stanford.library.sydney.edu.au., (2018). *Computer Ethics: Basic Concepts and Historical Overview (Stanford Encyclopedia of Philosophy/Spring 2006 Edition)*. [online] Available at: https://stanford.library.sydney.edu.au/archives/spr2006/entries/ethics-computer/ [Accessed 22 November 2018].
5. Thomson, A., & Schmoldt, D., (2001). *Ethics in Computer Software Design and Development* (pp. 85–102). [eBook] Elsevier. Available at: https://www.srs.fs.usda.gov/pubs/VT_Publications/01t7.pdf [Accessed 22 Nov. 2018].
6. West, D., (2018). *Why Tech Companies Need a Code of Ethics for Software Development*. [online] Entrepreneur. Available at: https://www.entrepreneur.com/article/311410 [Accessed 22 Nov. 2018].
7. Floridi, L., (2010). *The Cambridge Handbook of Information and Computer Ethics* (pp. 3–20). Cambridge: Cambridge University Press
8. Capurro, R. (2005). Privacy. An Intercultural Perspective. Ethics and Information Technology, 7(1), pp.37-47.
9. Rubin, R. and Froehlich, T. (2009). Ethical Aspects of Library and Information Science. Encyclopedia of Library and Information Sciences, Third Edition, pp.1743-1757.
10. Fallis, D. (2007). Information ethics for twenty□first century library

professionals. Library Hi Tech, 25(1), pp.23-36.

11. Forester, T. and Morrison, P. (1994). *Computer ethics*. Cambridge, Mass.: MIT Press.
12. Veatch, R. (1977). The Technical Criteria Fallacy. *The Hastings Center Report*, 7(4), p.15.

6

Cyberconflict and Ethics

CONTENTS

Cyberconflict" refers to actions that one state may initiate, purposefully, to cause damage to other states. It is important to have a legal structure in place within which the states should act so that the principles of humanity are upheld. There are various issues in cyberwarfare, and they are addressed in these chapters. The ACM code of ethics is a broad framework for IT professional that will enable them to discharge the duties with the moral guidelines. There are certain tools that can be employed to avoid cyberwarfare. But it is acknowledged that active defenses are important since it deters cyber attackers. Principles of international law of war should also be applied to cyberwar. The role of the UN Charter is also significant to minimize the threat of war, so that wide-spread collateral damage can be avoided. Parameters have been laid down on the basis of which the impact of the cyberwar can be assessed. With cyberwarfare spreading to more and more countries, the role of non-state actors in the cyberwarfare has increased, which has its own benefits and drawbacks. There are some legal aspects of this as well that needs to be considered. The law of proportionality is crucial to cyberwarfare which states that combatants and non-combatants should be clearly demarcated. With the internet spreading to more and more countries, hacktivism is also gaining ground. The impact of the same deserves consideration.

6.1. INTRODUCTION

Prima facie, most cyber-attacks can be unambiguously classified as illegal as well as immoral. Cyber-attacks also include those attacks that are carried out for bragging rights and pleasure. The most common cyber-attacks in the present world are the web defacements which are carried out "just for fun" and several other computer viruses which are mostly disregarded for their consequences.

At times it is also for unscrupulous motives like such as system intrusion to extract sensitive information, rob bank accounts; denial-of-service attacks intended to make network inaccessible to the intended users or extorting money from victims; and attacks that compromise and deploy large "botnets" of victim computers to send out spam or amplify denial-of-service attacks.

Ethical issues are vexed in primarily in three areas of cyberconflict. The first is cyberwarfare involving actions taken by the state to maintain national security. The first is cyberwarfare involving actions taken by the state to maintain national security. The first area in which the ethical issues are vexed is the cyber-warfare.

Cyberwarfare is performed at the state level which is approved by the national security. As cyber-warfare security is related to national security, there are several queries that are raised with regards to performing these cyber-attacks. Those questions include,

- If it is moral for a state to inactive and infiltrate an adversary's systems which have threatened its political and territorial integrity, if yes, to put forth the general rules and guideline to be followed to perform those attacks.
- The ways by which both, the electric power and the telecommunications department that serve the military functions and the civilian functions of a country be attacked by this cyber-warfare.
- Another significant question which was raised are the ways by which a country reacts to the cyber-attacks that are performed by another country.
- And if there are any chances that a country will be able to attack a third country whose computer networks have been compromised or exploited to facilitate the assault?

The second area where the ethical dilemma is faced involves acts that are carried out in the interest of a certain social cause or of a political party. "Hacktivism" is the term coined to represent this area of conflict since it signifies the convergence of hacking with activism.

If the attack is planned with the motive of causing significant harm to civilians and cause widespread terror, they are termed as "cyberterrorism." It is a term coined to signify the confluence of cyber-attacks with terrorism. Cyberterrorism can be unambiguously labeled as heinous and immoral; however, hacktivism raises ethical dilemmas. For instance: can a cyber-attack be considered as ethical when the hackers take down a website which is mainly used to trade child pornography, or a cyber-attack which supports terrorist operations or performing attacks on stolen credit card numbers trafficking.

The ways how a hacktivist who protest against the practices and policies that are framed by the government to deface a website or to perform a web "sit-in." The rights of a hacktivist to attack a vulnerable system which aids in disclosing the security holes which in turns aims in making the internet more secure.

The third area where the ethical dilemma is encountered is the ethics of cyberdefense, specifically known as the "strike back," "active response" or hack back." The third area of cyber defense also demonstrates the ways by which the system administrators (victims) react and respond to the attack and to know if the attack is coming from systems that may themselves be victims of compromise. As most of the cyber-attacks are directed through the chains of compromised machines, can a victim "hack back" along the chain in order to determine the source?

However, rather than exploring for answers to the above questions, this chapter details the various ethical issues in each of these areas of cyberconflict and create a framework by which all the questions can be addressed effectively.

With the help of examples, principles have been explained; however, the aim here is not to reach a final moral conclusion. That would require a much more detailed examination of the specific cyber-attack taking into account the motive and the background.

The framework presented here is based on the international law of armed conflict. This law was formulated to acknowledge and redress the threats of armed attacks and the usage of primarily armed force. However, some efforts have been channeled into making it relevant in the domain of cyberconflict. For a better understanding of the framework, the law has been segregated into two parts;

- jus ad bellum, or the law of conflict management; and
- jus in bello, or the law of war.

Despite being stated as "laws," the two segments of this law details more about the ethical behavior in a cyberconflict as these ethical behaviors act as the rules of law.

Ethics is a field of study that provides a guidance of what is right and what is wrong, governs a person's behavior and helps in taking a moral stand. Ethics primarily examines the morality of social structures, policies, laws, and human behaviors of a nation. The primary work of ethicists is to justify their moral judgments by reference to ethical principles of theories which tries to retain and capture the moral intuitions about what is right and wrong. The most common theoretical approaches are of two types, namely;

- Consequentialism; and
- Deontology.

As per the consequentialist approach, actions that lead to bad consequences can be termed as wrong. Whereas, deontological approaches assume that the moral duties of an individual have to be viewed independently of the consequence of their actions, whether good or bad.

Mostly, ethical principles and legislations are interconnected with each other. But it is found that it is not possible for a legislation to function as a substitute for morality. It is for this reason that individuals and corporations are always required to consider not only the legality but also the morality of their actions. Ethical analysis of privacy and security issues in the field of Information Technology (IT) took place primarily in computer ethics that emerged in the late 1980s.

The moral or ethical analysis should be included to address these ethical problems and questions: analysis aimed at a study of why certain issues can be termed as morally right or morally wrong and resolving the same and also reasoned views behind making these judgments. The aim of moral analysis is to provide clear knowledge and bring an equilibrium between several rights, interests, values. The moral analysis should also aid in evaluating policies and course of actions of those values which are at stake (Figure 6.1).

Figure 6.1: Cyber attacks and its threat have taken-over the IT industry.

Source:https://cdn.pixabay.com/photo/2017/10/14/17/32/cyber-security–2851201_960_720.jpg

6.2. CODES OF ETHICS

The study on the code of ethics provides a broader social consciousness of "Cause No Harm" and improves the quality of work which in turn reduces the dangerous outcomes. The code of ethics can be studied in detail under two categories, they are;

- Association for Computing Machinery (ACM); and
- Institute of Electrical and Electronics Engineers (IEEE).

According to Landau in 2008, "An ACM member shall consider the health, privacy, and general welfare of the public in the performance of the members work. An ACM member, when dealing with data concerning individuals, shall always consider the issue of individual privacy and seek the following: to minimize the data collection; to limit authorized access to data; To provide proper security for the data; to determine the required retention period of the data; to ensure proper disposal of the data."

The Institute for Certification of IT Professionals (ICCP) has a code of ethics IT professional have to adhere to. The code underlines the importance of possessing high standards of skill and knowledge, necessitates the maintenance of confidentiality, and that the IT professional will recognize the public reliance upon the standards of conduct and established practices. The code of ethics which the members of the Association of IT Professionals (AITP) are required to follow are:

- To promote management's understanding of information processing;
- To refrain from dishonest practices and act with dignity;
- Contribute to the best of their capacity in sharing IT knowledge;
- To maintain confidentiality;
- Base actions on ethical and moral principles that they have acquired in educational institutions;
- Be faithful to their employers and safeguard their interests; and
- To value their countries and the way of life of those countries.

The above seven values are the key concepts of the code of ethics that consist of justice, utility, respect for individuals, consistency, autonomy for all, integrity, and competence.

6.3. CYBERWARFARE

Instances of major cyber-attacks around the world have often prompted the various governments to shift the blame on other governments. Often there have been speculations of cyberwarfare breaking out. As defined by the Oxford English Dictionary "The use of computer technology to disrupt the activities of a state or organization, especially the deliberate attacking of information systems for strategic or military purposes."

The significance of the above definition is that the aim of cyberwarfare is not in attacking the neighboring countries with the use of computer-technologies, but it means that intra-national banks or any other actions which uses the computer system as a mode to launch a threat.

The biggest challenge that cyberwarfare poses is the difficulty to find out who could be the perpetrator of the attack. Some latest technologies and intelligence can expose the state or group that may have been responsible, but with intelligent use of technology, it is easy to cover up the identity, cover up the tracks from where hacks have sourced as well as mask the malware infections and other methods employed

Many freelance groups and hackers are recruited by the intelligence agencies and military operations to help them in attacking the target on their behalf. It becomes more challenging for the victims to identify the perpetrator to give them appropriate punishments for their criminal offenses (Figure 6.2).

Figure 6.2: Cyberwarfare: The dark side of cyberspace.

Source: https://c1.staticflickr.com/3/2911/33509637200_2834019633_b.jpg

6.3.1. Tools to Avoid Cyberwarfare

The weapons used to tackle cyberwarfare are identical to the ones primarily used in criminal attacks everywhere. So, there are DDoS botnets to serve up denial of service attacks which can interrupt if not actually take strategic servers out of play. DDoS is usually used as a resource in various data crimes in order to direct smokescreen for other activities on the network. Social engineering and spear phishing attacks are also weaponized to introduce an attacker into the system of an adversary. The insider threat is a very import weapon in the cyberwarfare armory, and so does having a mole to leak information.

Cybersecurity issues and challenges can be highlighted better with illustration to explain the subject in hand. However, it is not easy in case of state-sponsored attacks as the attack cannot be pinpointed to a specific person as explained above. There are several other illustrations that could be classified as cyberwarfare details and illustrates the kinds of attacks which shall be studied below.

The most obvious cyberwarfare is the Stuxnet, which was initially discovered in 2010. The Stuxnet cyberwarfare primarily involved Israel and the United States using a sophisticated worm to destroy nuclear centrifuges in Iran, so as to delay the progress of its nuclear weapons development program.

What happened in Russia can be taken as an example. The country has been suspected of carrying out numerous state-level cyber-attacks. It is facing the accusation of increasing cyber-attacks against Ukraine. Allegedly, it has used BlackEnergy attack that caused blackout to 70,000 houses in the country in 2015 and Not Petya malware, which was actually designed purely to damage the systems it infected but was impersonating a ransomware.

The most sort after topic which has been on headlines is the North Korea's nuclear posturing and turbulent diplomatic relationship with the US that also includes the active participation in cyberspace. According to researches, "the North Korean state has been linked to the prolific and dangerous hacking organization codenamed HIDDEN COBRA, also known as the Lazarus Group. Both the Sony hack of 2014 and the hack of a Bangladeshi bank in 2016 were pinned on these hackers."

6.3.2. Jus ad Bellum and Cyberconflict

What is a subject matter of contention is when a state can take steps to counter cyber-attacks in self-defense? The laws of war are well defined and comprise of widely accepted principles. However, the application of those principles is a challenge. Most of the law of war was developed to counter traditional war methods; hence their principles cannot apply to cyber-attacks in all scenarios.

In the paradigm of examining the armed attacks, the scope of an attack and the identification of an attacker has been easier when compared to other cyber-attacks. Generally, it becomes difficult for a state to assess the nature of cyber-attack when they are in process and becomes more challenging to identify the person responsible for the attack which has made states unwilling to react to those attacks in self-defense for fear of violating the law of war. This negligence of non-reactive nature to the attacks have turned cyberwarfare into one of the key topics in international law.

The crux of this chapter is to discover the unique challenges which the cyber-attacks pose to the law of war and provide the readers an analytical framework for dealing with them. Once the present state of the law of war are fully explored, this chapter will demonstrate that states have a right under international law to:

- Treat cyber-attacks as acts of war and not merely as criminal matters.
- Use defensive mechanism against computer networks, both active and passive, against states found guilty of initiating cyber-attacks. Also, states have a responsibility to counter attacks within their borders and will be held guilty even if there was passive involvement.

The key purpose of this chapter is to provide a deep understanding of the law of war. This chapter primarily deals in addressing the technical aspects of cyberwarfare also showcases the presence of legal body for every state which acts as a self-defense to these cyber-attacks.

The following are the seven principles of law of war which the U.S. Department of Defense summarizes; (DoD OGC)

- **Distinction of Combatants from Noncombatants:** The exclusive right to use force lies with the nation's armed force, and they must not mask their identity and hide behind civilians or in civilian properties;
- **Military Necessity:** The targets of the cyber-attacks should make a direct contribution to the war effort or produce a military

advantage;

- **Proportionality:** During an attack on a lawfully military target, if collateral damage to civilians and civilian properties is inevitable, the probable military advantage should be proportionate to the damage;
- **Indiscriminate Weapons:** Avoidance of using weapons which cannot be directed with any precision. An example for an indiscriminate weapon is the bacteriological weapon;
- **Superfluous Injury:** Abstain from using weapons that are likely to cause irrevocable losses and fatal injuries;
- **Perfidy:** Neither the symbols that are protected are not meant to be utilized to immunize the military targets from attacks, nor they are to be fake surrendered or issued false reports of cease-fires; and
- **Neutrality:** Countries are entitled to immunity from attack if they do not assist either side; else, they become legitimate targets.

Out of the above seven principles, the first three principles deal with the wars which are to only be performed by the military forces, and the primary focus of that attack should of military targets rather than civilian ones irrespective of the nature of attacks whether cyber or kinetic.

The consent to cyber-attack crucial infrastructures such as financial systems, civilian energy distribution, transportation, and telecommunication are permitted only if the attack do not cause disproportionate and redundant collateral damage to civilian property and noncombatants.

6.3.3. Proposals and Defenses

Active defenses are crucial to make the state cyberdefense measures effective. Also, it acts as a warning and a deterrent to cyber-attacks since the assailant would not want to deal with counterattack. For the purpose of using active defenses, the country should ensure a legal authority prior to performing a defense attack, which flows from the longstanding duty which mentions that the state is in a plight to prevent nonstate actors from using their territory to commit cross-border attacks.

Conventionally, the duty of the state is to deter illegal activities that the state has prior knowledge of. However, this duty has evolved in the background of international terrorism, and now states are also bound to act against groups with past records of illegal acts.

In the outburst of cyber-warfare, the duty of the state to deter illegal activities should be taken as a crucial concern, so as to formulate, enforce, and enact legal regulations which helps in declining the cross-border cyber-attacks. If the country does not aim in formulating the required measures to deter cyber-attacks, the present scenario which is being encountered by the United States with China and Russia will continue to exist. If states are demanded to enact and enforce criminal law against cyber-attacks, the current hostile situation will resolve itself because:

- Either the United States will violate their responsibility which aid in creating a constitutional trail for victim-states to hold them lawfully accountable for an attack without having to attribute it first. If a country is being constantly attacked by the attackers and the country fails to appropriate take action against its attackers, then this country is considered to be a "sanctuary state" permitting other countries to use active defenses against cyber-attacks originating from within its borders.

International laws should give guidelines to ensure appropriate usage of active defenses since employing active defenses is crucial. Due to the unpredictable nature of countries, it is important that the international law ensures in getting the States to act in a predictable way which makes the country more acceptable in the international community.

It is also crucial that the international law formulate rigid guidelines for the appropriate usage of active defenses which in turn would aid in minimizing the unpredictable and unacceptable responses to the cyber-attacks. The law of war is very powerful and is well capable of giving the required information to the states; a careful examination of the same is required for guidance.

As stated earlier, the law of warfare is divided into two segments which are just in bello and jus ad bellum, which is also called as the law of conflict management. The law of conflict management deals with the constitutional management that governs the transformation of a country between the war to peace.

Generally, the law of conflict demonstrates as to when the states may legally retort to an armed conflict. Another known law of armed conflict is the jus in bello which administers the exact use of forces during an armed war. To arrive at a decision of whether cyber-attacks should be countered with active defenses, jus ad bellum should be referred to by the state, since jus ad bellum defines the threshold beyond which cyber-attacks must be considered acts of war. Article 2(4) forbids states from retaining "the threat or use of force against the territorial integrity or political independence of [another] state, or in any other manner inconsistent with the Purposes of the United Nations." This article thus, forbids both active defense and also the threat of the aggressive use of force by states and considers it as crimes against international peace and security.

The United Nations Charter's protections started to rapidly spread, and several countries around the world started to implement the Article 2(4) as a customary international law even though this law was formulated only for the country's that are parties to it, which later resulted in combining all the countries across the world.

Only some exception can be referred to in the UN Charter, and states can threaten to use active defense or make use of force against another state. This position is further supported by Article 2(3), which requires states to "settle their international disputes by peaceful means in such a manner that international peace and security, and justice, are not endangered."

6.4. UN SECURITY COUNCIL ACTIONS AND CYBER-CONFLICTS

There are certain set of exceptions which every country has to adhere to during the cyberconflicts. The actions that are authorized by the United Nations Security Council is the foremost exception to the common exclusion on the use of forces.

In order to restore and maintain global peace and security, the Security Council can make use of the article 42 of the United Nations Charter which are primarily to be used through the military forces of a country. However, unless the Security Council fulfills the conditions of articles 39, 41, and 42, the Security Council is not entrusted the power to use the military forces under the United Nations Charter.

Article 39 must be examined first before the Security Council can sanction the use of force. Article 39 requires the existence of "threat to the peace, breach of the peace, or act of aggression" which is to be determined by the Security Council. It is only when the above criteria are fulfilled, the Security Council has got the power to initiate in restoring the global peace and security which should be in line with the Articles 41 and 42 of the United Nations Charter.

Article 41 that provides guidance on the use of nonmilitary measures is Charter's favored method to restore international peace and security. Under this article, the Security Council has the power to administer a country for the usage of nonmilitary measures to coerce an offending country into ceasing its aggression. The members of the United Nations are responsible in implementing the nonmilitary measures, which includes the "complete or partial interruption of economic relations, and other means of communication, and the severance of diplomatic relations."

When the measures under Article 41 have not been effective or is not expected to be successful, military measures under Article 42 may be sanctioned by the Security Council. Although Article 41 authorizes the Security Control to impose the use of non-military forces, but a state cannot be forced to take military action invoking Article 42, it can only authorize the state to do so.

As discussed, the use of force is prohibited under normal circumstances. However, another exception to this restriction is when force is required to be used for self-defense. The Article 51 of the UN Charter confers this right. This article asserts that "nothing in the present Charter shall impair the inherent right of [states to engage in] individual or collective self-defense" in response to an "armed attack." Self-defense was considered a righteous act even before the UN Charter, and this fact has been implied in Article 51 as well.

The UN Charter also endorsed this right under the customary international law. The fundamental principle of self-defense is the right to survive is cardinal to all states and states may employ force to safeguard themselves and their citizens.

This right is independent of the UN Charter. Hence self-defense analysis borrows from the principles customary international law and the provisions of Article 51.

The essence of the principle of self-defense is that it may be resorted to when faced with a threat of armed attack. Although this principle is accepted and acknowledged by the international law, the question of what constitutes an armed attack is yet to be settled. This lack of clarity has led to the deliberation over when a state has the right to retaliate under self-defense.

It is vital that self-defense is invoked at the right time, hence the dispute of what can be termed as armed attack, needs to be settled. In case of cyber-attacks, there can be more than one interpretation, unlike traditional warfare weapons. Hence the debate on what can be classified as armed attack has become more prominent. Self-defense analysis is further complicated because of competing theories among legal scholars on the interplay between the UN Charter and customary international law. Some scholars favor UN Charter. Their argument is that Article 51 places a restriction on self-defense since it allows the same only to respond against an actual armed act. While others emphasize on customary international law.

Their argument is that the states have every right to be proactive and retaliate against impending armed attacks as well. Imminent armed attacks have been deliberated later. The important point here is although different philosophies have come up with various descriptions of an armed attack, there is a common agreement over the fact that once a state is attacked with armed forces by another state, the victim states and its allies have the legal authority to use force against the perpetrator.

Methods employed for self-defense must obey the international law. An armed attack does not automatically empower the victim state to start unrestricted war against the perpetrator. Self-defense should be resorted to only when it is necessary and when it cannot be avoided because alternative peaceful methods have been deemed ineffective in the prevailing circumstances. Self-defense should be conducted in proportion to the armed attack. Self -defense actions should be restricted to the amount of force deemed necessary to thwart any advances or to overthrow an ongoing attack.

This principle in no way states that the magnitude and extent of defense should be comparable to those of the attack. In self-defense, a state may employ force of greater magnitude if it is required to deter the attacker. The chief consideration here is to determine the amount of force, to either tackle the present hostile situation or to prevent future attacks from happening. The above-mentioned principles set out the boundaries within which the responses must confirm.

The UN Charter lays down the condition that a state may only use force against another state when it is compelled to do so to defend itself or under the auspices of the Security Council (Article 39). The Charter has been successful in laying down a moral principle of a justified reason when a state can attack another state, and this has been accepted universally. States are only empowered to safeguard themselves from threats of violence or actual aggression.

They do not have the right to initiate attack without any ground. The use of force can be allowed only as a defense mechanism against aggression. The application of these moral and legal principles to cyberwarfare is only possible after it is concluded without reasonable doubt that the cyber-attacks employed force. If they are classified as armed attack, it would come under the purview of UN Charter. Cyber-attacks at the state level would then be considered morally right as an act of self-defense. But if they are not classified as a form of force, moral issues regarding their use is very unclear, falling closer to the issues raised by "softer" forms of coercion such as trade restrictions and severance of diplomatic relations.

6.5 USE OF FORCE AND CYBERATTACK

Cyber-attacks around the world are not identical. The impact of cyber-attack that cause electricity blackout for one hour is less severe when compared to one that causes planes to crash by scrambling air traffic signals Thus there is a necessity to have a framework for assessing a particular attack or class of attacks to conclude whether the use of armed force is justified.

In 1999, Michael Schmitt, professor of international law and Director of the Program in Advanced Security Studies at the George G. Marshall European Center for Security Studies in Germany offered seven principles which differentiated the operations which use the forces from diplomatic, economic, and other soft measures.

The high end resembling the use of force and the low end resembling soft measures are the key spectrum of consequences when those seven criteria are segregated into one criterion. The description of seven criteria is based on the work of both the authors of international law conflict, Thomas Wingfield and Schmitt.

- **Severity**: It refers to the damage to life and property. It denotes that wide-spread calamity, loss of life and damage to property is caused due to armed attacks, but soft measures do not have such consequences.
- **Immediacy**: It refers to the time that it takes for the effect of the attacks to be felt. Generally, it is seen that the effects of use of armed forces are immediate, often within seconds or minutes, while in case of softer measures, like imposing bans, the consequences are felt much later, often after weeks or months.
- **Directness**: The association between an operation and the effects of operation is known as directness. Generally, the effects for an armed attack are caused by and attributable to the application

of force, whereas for softer measures there could be multiple explanations.

- **Invasiveness**: Those armed attacks which comprises of physical cross borders into the target country is known as invasiveness. Concurrently, softer measures are implemented from within the borders of a sponsoring country.
- **Measurability**: This refers to the ability to quantify the effects of an operation. The basis is that the impact of armed attacks can be more readily measured like the number of deaths, the value of impairment to wealth, etc. than softer measures, for example, trade restrictions.
- **Presumptive Legitimacy:** Presumptive legitimacy is the validation of an operation to be genuine in the global community. Whereas the use of armed force is generally unlawful absent some justifiable reason such as self-defense, the use of soft measures is generally lawful absent some prohibition.
- **Responsibility:** Responsibility refers to the degree to which the consequence of an action can be attributed to a state as opposed to other actors. In case of use of armed force, the state can be directly held responsible as it is the exclusive province of the state hence can be attributed directly to it, whereas non-state actors are capable of getting themselves involved in such soft activity as propaganda and boycotts.

Let us consider an example to understand how these criteria would apply to a cyber-attack. A cyberintrusion on air traffic control has resulted in two large aircraft to enter the same airspace and collide. The effects of crash have been devastating leading to the loss of 500 lives on board of these two aircraft.

Responsibility comes out moderate to high. In theory, the crime could be committed by anyone. But most hackers would not have the required skill and information. Only a state could possess such resources. In summary, five criteria such as immediacy, directness, presumptive, measurability, and legitimacy are ranked high, whereas two criteria such as responsibility and invasiveness are ranked at least moderate. Thus, apparently, the attack is not a soft measure or a legitimate form of coercion but a more severe application of force (Figure 6.3).

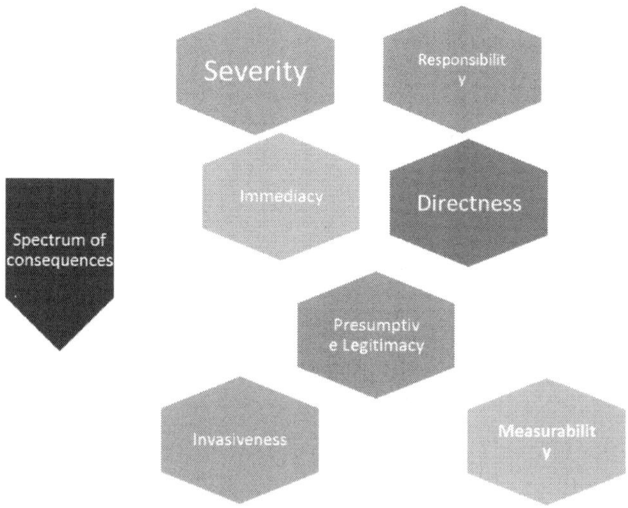

Figure 6.3: *Spectrum of consequences.*

6.6. NON-STATE ACTORS AND ITS INCREASE IN CYBERWARFARE

Armed forces and intelligence around the world have recognized the urgency to rapidly achieve a military cyberspace operation capability since the cyberwarfare has started to spread to more and more countries. During the year 2013, the Department of Defense of the U.S. sanctioned a major expansion of its Cybercommand.

Consequently, its size multiplied fivefold to almost 5000 troops and civilians. For well-developed nations the priority would be to build defensive capability, securing susceptible digital resources, such as command and control systems. Whereas developing countries may identify cyberspace operations as a striking technique of warfare, owing to the fact that is relatively low-cost method, and low risk-from from a political perspective to engage in a war against an opponent with kinetic battlefield dominance.

Cyberwarfare is expected to involve a plethora of methods. It could include destruction of vital infrastructures, cause critical injuries and loss to human lives, psychological techniques that could be disruptive. Other methods include creating confusion which would lead to information warfare and create uncertainty among their opposition. The character of cyber-attack is such that it can strike both strategic and tactical targets from great distances. Additionally, the technology involved is also less expensive.

However, the drawbacks of using cyber-attacks are substantial. The downside to it is the lack of control over the extent of collateral damage and calculation of value of the same in the targeting process, whereas the data is more readily available in case of conventional warfare. The cyberspace is a highly sophisticated and interdependent in nature.

This makes it difficult to assess whether an attack in this space will not only cause disruptions in the military network but also cause collateral damage to civilians, non-combatant or possibly the person who is carrying out the attacks himself. Hence the political risk needs to be taken into consideration, and this is often high. The unintended consequences may cause conflict escalation, carries the risk of making the cause look less legitimate in front of the international community, receive negative responses from their own people and augment resistance in the nation that was attacked. These shortcomings will deter nations-states from using cyber-attacks.

6.6.1. Actors Involved in Cyberwarfare

Table 6.1: Main Non-State Actors in Cyberconflict

Actor	**Motivation**	**Target**	**Method**
Ordinary citizens	None (or weak)	Any	Indirect
Script kiddies	Curiosity, thrills, ego	Individuals, companies, governments	Previously written scripts and tools
Hacktivists	Political or social change	Decision makers or innocent victims	Protests via web page defacements or DDoS attacks
Black-hat hackers	Ego, personal animosity, economic gain	Any	Malware, viruses, vulnerability exploits
White-hat hackers	Idealism, creativity, respect for the law	Any	Penetration testing, parching
Grey-hat hackers	Ambiguous	Any	Varying
Patriot hackers	Patriotism	Adversaries of own nation-state	DDoS attacks, defacements

Cyber insiders	Financial gain, revenge, grievance	Employer	Social engineering, backdoors, manipulation
Cyber terrorists	Political or social change	Innocent victims	Computer-based violence or destruction
Malware authors	Economic gain, ego, personal animosity	Any	Vulnerability exploits
Cyber scammers	Financial gain	Individuals, small companies	Social engineering
Organized cyber-criminals	Financial gain	Individuals, companies	Malware for fraud, identity theft, DDoS for blackmail
Corporations	Financial gain	ICT-based systems and infrastructures (private or public)	Range of techniques for attack or influence operations
Cyber espionage agents	Financial and political gain	Individuals, companies, governments	Range of techniques to obtain information
Cyber militias	Patriotism, professional development	Adversaries of own nation-state	Based on the group capabilities

Source: https://www.researchgate.net/publication/310827486_Non-State_Actors_in_Cyberspace_Operations/download

6.6.2. Employment of Non-State Actors in Cyberworld

In traditional methods of warfare can be attributed to a particular state. In case of cyberspace, anonymity can be maintained, and to a large extent, perpetrators can carry out attacks without the risk of being exposed. While employing a non-state actor in a cyber-world, the nation-states inclined to have very little or no backup in binding definition of cyberwar. This employment of non-state actors also tends to restrict the liberty to take any action or to formally take responsibility for executed cyber attacks.

Additionally, in cyber-attacks, there is less drainage of resources and is believed that it can cause severe disruptions or at least cause disturbances to ICT-based services.

Table 6.2: Benefits and Drawbacks of Using Non-State Actors in Cyberspace Operations

Benefits	Drawbacks
Gaining the initiative – element of surprise	No direct control of non-state actors
Plausible deniability	Risk of unintended collateral damage
Can choose target and attack vector	Targeting of own resources
Determinate scale and duration of attack	Escalation to conventional war
Exploit legal uncertainties	Labeling as sponsor of terrorism
Possibility of rapid attacking-by-proxy	Backlashes (blackmailing etc.)

Source: https://www.researchgate.net/publication/310827486_Non-State_Actors_in_Cyberspace_Operations/download

The above table gives a keynote of some of the significant "benefits and drawbacks" of performing a cyberwarfare, and how the employment of non-state actors is associated in the cyberspace operations.

Benefits of Using Non-State Actors:

- The primary advantage for an attacker is that the attacks can be performed in a much-secured way which can result in huge surprises or high possibility of uncertainty. As the attacker is in a position of initiating the attack, the options left with the defender are only to respond to those attacks, which are mostly predicted by the attacker.
- The attacker has the advantage of precision of time, and the ability to choose the specific target as per their own picking, using attack methods that are most suitable. For an attacker to perform an attack, not many processes or systems are needed other than a computer system. On the other hand, a victim would require several protections or defense systems in order to overcome a cyber-attack. The defense materials that are required to shield the victim's computer systems are exorbitantly expensive.
- The attacker can decide how to attack and the scale and duration of attack to have the desired impact. The responsibility of the attack can also be entrusted to a third party. This way they can amplify the impact of the act and also not risk direct attribution.
- Even if the accused is identified by the victim and the attack can be

attributed to the perpetrator, the absence of relevant international laws applicable is a loophole that can be successfully used to create a shield of legal ambiguity.

- It is not only that an attacker should perform an attack. There are chances that the attack could be outsourced to the organized cybercriminals, mercenary hackers or the cyber militias. This recruitment of third parties or the non-state actors tend to increase the doubt in the global community; however, the absence of proofs will shield the attacker political ramifications. Thus, making it challenging to for the victims to perform a counterstrike on the attackers.
- It becomes less expensive for an employer, if a non-state actor is recruited who have had previously identified Internet forums and social networks, technically competent force, suitably motivated, and rapid mobilization of a considerable to perform these attacks.

Drawbacks of Using Non-State Actors:

- The attacker may not be in total control of non-state actors in cyberspace operations, even though he commands what targets and methods should be employed during the cyber-attack, as there is little control over undesirable behavior, and it is difficult to end ongoing attacks.
- Attacks may extend beyond the desired scope and size. The attacker may accidentally hit targets that were not planned and cause undesired collateral damage. Excessively keen associates of cyber cities, not limited by the limitations that govern military organizations, could opt to target civilian targets without any thought of possible consequences.
- Common infrastructures like Internet backbone connections, may get overloaded which would adversely impact the attacker's network and resources if attack non-state actors are engaged.
- In the case where an attack is diverted against the systems of the civilians, the attacker and their nation could be accused of sponsoring for cyberterrorism or could be accused of committing war crimes, becoming pariah as far as international relations are concerned.
- If attacks are attributed to the initiating nation-state, the political impact would be disastrous, even though the laws of war are

ambiguous regarding cyberspace. If matters are escalated, the attacker state may have to face warfare through traditional means.

- Although the immediate attacks that are performed by the non-state actor tends to be successful, in the long run, these attackers are not tend to be reliable. These attackers, over a period of time, might blackmail a public administration, forcing the government officials to expose the complex details relating to the nation and contracted cyber espionage agents might defect to the opposing nation if offered political asylum.

6.6.3. Legal Issues Related to Non-State Actors in Cyberworld

The cyberwarfare has to deal with many legal challenges especially those pertaining to frameworks within which the present state-to-state operate. The main emphasis of this chapter is not on in-depth analysis of quirks and twists of international law. However, the current ambiguity in the prevailing legislation and international conventions do deserve mention, and to discern the impact of this uncertainty on employment of non-state actors in state-sponsored cyberconflict.

If cyber-attacks is resorted to, it will be against the spirit of the Law of Armed Conflict, even if it cannot be considered as a breach of the precept of war. Even other damaging cyber actions of less gravity may also be classified as acts of war by the UN Charter. Consequently, the UN Charter may authorize legitimate use of force in self-defense.

An important point to remember is that for an act to be categorized as cyber-attack, it should include violence or the possibility of the act becoming violent. This ambiguity prevents the classification of cyberspace as a combat zone. Consequently, many it would serve the interest of many nations if the laws of warfare are not applied to cyberwarfare.

Another point to note is that cyber-attacks cannot be carried out while confirming to laws and regulations. It is challenging to carry out the attacks within the ambit of the legal framework.

However, if the revised protocol on cyberwarfare is endorsed worldwide, nations may consider carrying out cyber-attacks through cyber-militias. This can be a feasible option since cyber-militias are known to undertake outsourced jobs of this nature.

Unfortunately, international laws have not been amended yet, and they remain ambiguous about the status of cyberwarfare. The attacker seems to have the upper hand, and the victims remain at the receiving end with very little means of retaliating.

Another pertinent question arises regarding the status of the individual who carries out a cyber attack and whether he can earn the distinguished status of a combatant. The Third Geneva Convention confers two types of status on a combatant namely privileged and unprivileged.

Privileged combatants are considered a part of the armed forces who are a party to the conflict. They enjoy the following privileges,

(I) they follow the orders of a superior who is responsible for people under him;

(ii) Carry distinguishing identification that can be recognized even from a distance;

(iii) They are permitted to carry arms with not attempt to conceal them;

(iv) They have to carry out operations within the dictate of laws of war.

Most non-state actors like hackers, criminals, and terrorists evidently, do not strictly adhere to this purview. One argument is that when a state sponsors a cyber-attacker or cyberespionage agents, these agents obey the orders of a superior who is responsible for their actions. However, it is very clear that these groups do not wear a fixed distinct sign that can be identified nor, do they carry arms blatantly. Besides, many of their activities can be classified as a breach of the laws and customs of war.

The requirements set out in the in the Geneva Convection may not be met, even by the regular military cyber force. Also, being a part of cyberwarfare could be detrimental to them, since the privileged combatant status awarded to them could be revoked. Members of the armed may carry out cyber-attacks in uniforms, but it will not be visible to the victims. There is very less possibility of carrying arms blatantly as most cyber-attacks cannot be traced to their original source even if they are exposed.

Combatants should not breach laws of war or engage in actions that are in violation of the same. Actions like causing harm to civilians will rip off the special combatant status of the attacker. This inhibits the use of commercial infrastructure for the purpose of cyber-attacks, in paper at least. While privileged combatants deserve the same treatment as a prisoner of war, unprivileged combatants may be tried under the civilian laws of the nation that has detained them and may be punished under the same.

Attackers may not always abide by the laws of war in order to gain privileged combatant status. They may not be encouraged to because it is implausible that they might fall into the enemy hands. This holds true since the victims are unaware of the status of the combatant who initiated the attack. The situation can be compared to attacks using weapons that can be used from a great distance such as unmanned aerial vehicle (UAV) and intercontinental ballistic missiles (ICBM) since in the case of the latter too it is difficult to trace the attacks. However, these weapons are not that discrete and can reveal the identity of the nation instigating the attack. But in case of cyber weapons anonymity is almost certain.

Even if the non-state actor to whom the attack has been outsourced can be traced back to the instigator state, the connection does not make the attacker a combatant as per legal status. We can take the cyber-conflict between Russia and Georgia as an example. In these attacks that were carried out in August 2008, evidence pointed towards the website "StopGeorgia.ru" which carried instructions against Georgia to Kremlin.

Russian intelligence services (GRU) and "Nashi" a youth association were the mediums used for giving the commands. This led to the suspicion that the Russian government outsourced the task to non-state "hacktivist" to accomplish its goals. Even if we take into account that individual hacktivist may be supported by a nation-state, they cannot be granted the legal status of combatant. They would still be considered as cybercriminals.

Taking all things in consideration, this conflict between Russia and Georgia displayed a practical model for conducting low impact cyberattacks. The government could achieve at least a part of its tactical goals without the conceding proof of the attack being state-sponsored. This was possible because the instigating-state employed the services of patriot hackers or cyber-militias, through informal routes appealing to nationalist fervor.

The actual character of cyberwarfare and the status of actors participating in these activities is ambiguous and has been heavily guarded by employing abstruse terms in media and literature. Politicians also sensationalize these terms and leave a lingering idea that these concepts are unique in their nature. Cyberwarfare lacks solid empirical datasets and requires advancement in technologies that can be applied to the art of war.

It is important to acknowledge the presence of various non-state actors in cyberspace and their role in state-sponsored cyber-attacks. There may be no clear-cut distinction between these actors. It will be difficult to differentiate between script kiddies, cybercriminals, and cyberespionage agents or between cyber militias and patriot hackers as the distinction is indistinct. Likewise, multiple engagements can be undertaken by individual actors. Nevertheless, it is important to distinguish between the actors for the purpose of analysis.

There is a significant chance that this arena will have gain more prominence in the coming years, as internet becomes ubiquitous throughout the developing countries of Asia and Africa, due to these asymmetric advantages that may be leveraged in cyberspace. The crucial infrastructures of these countries will also evolve in the process. Cyber-attacks that are carried out with a political motive will be much more intense both in scale and number of incidences. Further, these attacks may not be linked to the perpetrator because the internet can guard identity.

The upsurge in the number of Internet users globally, problematic cyber activities engaged by state actor like cyber scammers and script kiddies will also grow. These users can create a lot of annoyance due to the following reasons:

- Firstly, the number of users in this group that are keen on misusing the cyberspace resources for personal motive is high.
- Secondly, there are a number of tools at disposal to exploit loopholes in security.
- Thirdly, the society is not conscious of the measures that have to be taken to secure information.

6.7. RESPONDING TO INTERNATIONAL CYBERATTACKS AS ACTS OF WAR: PROPORTIONALITY

A state that is engaged in war has to distinguish between combatants and noncombatants as per the principle of distinction. This principle can be perceived as two interrelated duties. The first principle is that the civilian population should be clearly demarcated from their forces. Secondly, before the onset of the attack, the superiors should not keep clear demarcation between civilian or civilian objectives and military objectives.

The Article 57.1 of the Protocol Additional to the Geneva Conventions of 12 August 1949 also enforces certain restrictions on certain persons "those who plan or decide upon an attack." In this chapter, they have been referred to as commanders.

- The commander's first duty is to "do everything feasible to verify that the objectives to be attacked are neither civilians nor civilian objects."
- The commander also has the duty to "take all feasible precautions in the choice of means and methods of attack with a view to avoiding, and in any event to minimizing, incidental loss of civilian life, injury to civilians and damage to civilian objects."
- The commander should not instigate any attack "which may be expected to cause incidental loss of civilian life, injury to civilians, damage to civilian objects, or a combination thereof, which would be excessive in relation to the concrete and direct military advantage anticipated."

It is important to note that, the concept of proportionality does not in any way place a constraint on commanders from causing any civilian death or injuries or destruction to civilian property. Proportionality states that loss to life and property should not exceed when compared to the "concrete and direct military advantage contemplated."

The principle of proportionality prohibits an attack if it is anticipated that expected damage to civilian lives and destruction of civilian property would outweigh the military gain contemplated from such an attack. In order to analyze proportionality, the direct military advantage should be evaluated against the destruction of civilian life and property.

6.8. CAUSES OF HACKTIVISM

Jus ad bellum to lays down the operations that states are prohibited from initiating against each other in the normal course of events, i.e., operations in which force is employed. Similarly, it is in the domain of domestic laws to place restrictions on operations that non-state actors can conduct.

The United States has laws governing cyber-attacks are contained in Title 18, Section 1030 of the U.S. Code (at the federal level) and in state computer crime laws.

These laws place a restriction on most of the cyber-attacks like web defacements, use of viruses, network intrusion, etc. Jus ad bellum permits states to engage in operations that employ force to in order to retaliate, that may otherwise have been termed as illegitimate. Domestic legal doctrine includes a concept of self-defense that permits the use of force by victims that in other circumstances would be considered illegal. Cyber-attacks can also be used as self-defense mechanism, and this aspect has been discussed later. There are some ethical grounds on which cyber-attacker can engage for political or social causes. Hacktivism may be ethically acceptable in cases like civil disobedience where laws and demands of the government are defied but through peaceful means. Civil disobedience is a means to raise objection, show dissent and highlight those laws policies and practices that are considered immoral or unfair.

The methods employed for civil disobedience includes demonstrations, barriers, trespass, etc. It involves defying law but is not necessarily accompanied by unethical actions. All civil disobedience movements cannot be automatically termed as moral but, in some cases, it may cross that boundary. For instance, the blocking of the entry point of an emergency room in a hospital to raise voice against the government's health care policy.

We can take the example of the Electronic Disturbance Theater (EDT). EDT promoted the application of electronic civil disobedience, mainly through "web sit-ins," which were viewed as virtual forms of physical sit-ins and blockades. Each sit-in would choose one or more websites as targets at a particular time and date and was updated in the public-forum in advance.

The activist has to go to a website to join the movement and select a target. Flood Net which is a Java applet would get downloaded in their computers so that the targeted website will get some traffic. A single participants' traffic would have insignificant impact on the website that is targeted; however, the collective traffic of thousands of participants, if they participate, could create havoc in the target website.

EDT had primarily used their web sit-ins to protest against the adverse policies of Mexican and U.S. government that had an impact on the Chiapas. Though initially EDT was used to express solidarity with the Mexican Zapatistas but later they also fought for numerous other causes. This idea also found acceptance among other groups like the U.K. based Electro Hippies.

With web sit-ins gaining popularity, the software tools employed became more sophisticated. Some of the software's used included ones that could be loaded into the target's system in advance and later be operated from participant's system, software that would be activated by active participation of the person involved.

It is important to determine the legality of hacktivism movements like web sit-ins. In this case, Schmitt's criteria can be used to assess whether a cyber-attack employs force or does it use soft and legitimate measures. Some of the legitimate measures include letter writing, speaking out, lobbying, petitions, etc. Schmitt's criteria rank these measures low on the use of force.

They cannot be termed as severe as the impairment is negligible. Also, to measure the impact is a challenge since their effects are not immediate or direct. They do not involve any illegitimate methods. The ease with which it can be performed makes them low on responsibility.

Most web defacements violate computer crime statutes. Schmitt's criteria can be used to assess web defacements. This would yield the result that it is high on four criteria- directness, presumptive legitimacy, measurability, and directness. It is easy to restore websites from back up; hence it is not that severe. But the damage could be high in cases like where a visitor makes use of incorrect medical information, or the security of online bank transaction is compromised, or the reputation of the enterprise owning the website is lost. Intrusiveness and responsibility can be ranked as moderate and low respectively. There are very few nations that claim to be responsible when they employ these methods. Web defacement cannot be performed by everyone; however, there is no dearth of hackers who can.

It can be deduced that, apparently, defacements are even less legitimate that web sit-ins and are certainly despised by many hacktivists.

Other types of hacktivism can also be scrutinized through Schmitt's criteria. Generally, actions that breach computer crime statutes are ranked moderate to high. Example of such cyber-attacks are actions to deter a child pornography site, attacks that aim to pint out and rectify lapses in security systems. Even though the end objective may be ethical, the methods employed may be disputed.

Any act that can be classified as cyberterrorism would have a very serious outcome even in the best-case scenario. Cyber-attacks that do not breach crime laws are ranked low as per Schmitt's criteria. For instance, developing new software and employing them in letter writing campaigns or innovating software for obtaining censored information by breaching its firewalls.

These activities cannot be considered illegal at least in the US and cannot be compared to the use of force. Cyber-attacks that are classified in upper ranges of Schmitt's criteria may require more justification but cannot be termed immoral. One factor to be considered is whether a possibility exists to achieve the activist's goals by actions which are within the ambit of law. Evaluating the case of defacement for protesting the CDA, it can be inferred that the hacker could have conveyed the information on his own website or used another party's website lawfully. This approach would have given the message a longer "shelf life."

REFERENCES

1. Arquilla, J., (2012). Conflict, security and computer ethics. *The Cambridge Handbook of Information and Computer Ethics* (pp. 133–148). [online]. Available at: https://www.cambridge.org/core/books/cambridge-handbook-of-information-and-computer-ethics/conflict-security-and-computer-ethics/4BAA5CC4ACEA0FEBA962A7F2167877AD [Accessed 15 Nov. 2018].
2. Brey, P., (2007). *Ethical Aspects of Information Security and Privacy*. [eBook] Available at: https://ethicsandtechnology.eu/wp-content/uploads/downloadable-content/Brey_2007_Information_Security.pdf [Accessed 15 Nov. 2018].
3. Carr, J., & Sklerov, J. M., (2018). *Inside Cyberwarfare, Responding to International Cyberattacks as Acts of War*. [online] O'Reilly | Safari. Available at: https://www.oreilly.com/library/view/inside-cyber-warfare/9781449318475/ch04.html [Accessed 15 Nov. 2018].
4. Denning, D., (n.d.). The Ethics of Cyberconflict. *The Handbook of Information and Computer Ethics* (pp. 407–428). [online]. Available at: https://www.researchgate.net/publication/228018156_The_Ethics_of_Cyber_Conflict [Accessed 15 Nov. 2018].
5. Morton, O. G., (2013). *Cyberspace Operations, Stuxnet, Jus Ad Bellum and Jus in Bello*. [eBook] Available at: http://www.dtic.mil/dtic/tr/fulltext/u2/1018827.pdf [Accessed 15 Nov. 2018].
6. Sigholm, J., (2013). Non-state actors in cyberspace operations. *Journal of Military Studies*, [online] *4*(1), pp. 1–37. Available at: https://www.researchgate.net/publication/310827486_Non-State_Actors_in_Cyberspace_Operations [Accessed 15 Nov. 2018].
7. Titiriga, R., (2011). *Cyber-Attacks and International Law of Armed Conflicts: A 'Jus Ad Bellum' Perspective*.

7

Technologies of Autonomous Agency

CONTENTS

The different aspects related to the development of computers and the way they changed the phase of technology along with the impact they have on the social and privacy of human lives have been discussed. The need for the innovation in technology along with the threats it has to the privacy and security of the users has been discussed in detail. The different types of autonomous agents, their characteristics, classification, and relation to the surroundings they live in have been elucidated. The risks from the cyber-attack and the different types of cyber-attacks have been explained. The legal framework and different laws with respect to the cybercrime have been explained.

7.1. INTRODUCTION, OR HOW TO DO ETHICS OF IT NOW?

The major aspect is to understand the technologies that are made by using a group of choices that are evolved from certain strategies that are constantly improved for successful execution which will result in a new technology. The different aspects that are considered in terms of technology that need to be considered are the different algorithms, codes, different top0logies, different monitoring systems, and various aspects that are related to the autonomous technologies along with the different policies and governing bodies that are used in terms of the different autonomous technologies.

The current world is completely global with networks and relationships being the vital aspect, which is based on a set of algorithms that decide the distance that messages need to travel to reach into networks. This distance is suggested based on the search history and preferences by filtering the different data according to several prerequisites. Digital technology decides the type of communication-based on rational thought process and visualization.

Eminent people like Eli Pariser in the year 2011 and other people like Epstein and Robertson have provided various descriptions in terms of these technologies by explaining several concepts such as Search Engine Manipulation effects (2015) with several examples. The technology that is being used is thus not neutral, as this technology is widely influenced by the different opinions that are present across the world and the different theories that are existing regarding the different autonomous technologies that are influenced by the behavior and thinking of different users.

There are a number of computer technologies that have come up in the recent times such as the tablets, laptops, and smartphones along with multiple novel software, applications, user interfaces and other default settings that form different our 'choice architectures' (Thaler and Sunstein, 2010) and our 'extended minds' (Clark and Chalmers, 1998). The different uncertainties and ethical aspects are challenged by a set of operations that control the programs that are executed.

There are several thought processes and research in different moral values and ethical considerations that need to incorporate into different technologies. The whole process of research and development is focusing on different ethical and moral aspects as there are a lot of novel and beautiful innovations that were withdrawn, just because they were not able to meet the ethical and moral constraints. Therefore, the computer ethics and moral considerations are an important aspect of any novel technology, and these are integral aspects of any research and development.

The different aspects of research and development are making major studies into different moral and ethical aspects that are pertaining to certain technologies. The ethics and moral values of every technology are dynamic, and they change based on different aspects such as the geography, region, climate, and culture. Therefore, there is need for adequate research for different moral and ethical aspects that can change the whole process of development of a technology.

There are two different aspects of the moral considerations that must be made in the field of information technology (IT), and they are:

- Initial factor being "a value turns in engineering design"; and
- Second factor that is "a design turns in thinking about values."

The computers were initially introduced in the mid-twentieth century with the focus on technology, and not much thought was given to them:

- The different applications of the computer in the real life;
- The use of computers in varied aspects of life;
- The impact that computers would have on the social, organizational, and political aspects of the society.

Computers were novel and interesting technological machines which have answers to a variety of problems. This marks the role and importance of value sensitive design (VSD) in the development of autonomous technologies which is "context-free," "context-independent" and "neutral." The early years of seventies and eighties were technology dominant, and these years people focused on the development of technologies, whereas these years the development of any technology is focusing on the moral and ethical implications.

The various aspects of social and behavioral sciences started increasing their focus on the different aspects of IT in the form of:

- Communication between the computer and human beings;
- The engineering model and design that is used in the development of the technology; and
- Various other aspects of social informatics.

The ethical and moral aspects of the technology were initially focused on a smaller set of values such as user-friendliness and the worker safety, however these days there a lot of ethical and moral aspects that needs to be researched and understood carefully before bringing up a technology. There is need to identify the possible barriers and risks and understand the implications of bringing up a technology.

The initial decade of the twenty-first century was mainly focused on the effective application of the principles of IT to the computers. This made the human beings completely dependent on the computers for various functions. Human beings, whether in their role as employers, consumers, citizens, or patients, have moral values, moral preferences, and moral ideals.

IT needs to support to human beings and must not be posing hurdles or challenges to the human beings. There are a lot of debates and arguments that are happening in terms of privacy, safety, liability, equality, autonomy, and accountability. The effective execution is largely interpreted based on the interference of the values in the process of design and architecture of systems.

Values are the integral part of development of technology in the twenty-first technology. The values can either be ethical values or moral values that play an important role in the development of technology. The values have entered a third stage of development of the IT which is referred to as "The Value Turn in IT" which incorporates the different values that are related to users, patients, and other citizens who are all a part of the development of a technology.

The development in the ethics and importance to the ethical aspects of technology has risen as a subject in the recent centuries and importance the different ethical terms like the "good" and "ought" to be being used in the recent times. The ethical aspects of technology must be given due importance and must be studied at several levels to make a technology that can survive and be used.

There were a lot of moral philosophers who began to read, observe, and understand the problems related to social policies and community debates. There were remarkable developments in the United States that enabled the understanding that philosophy supports, social, and political constraints that could influence the different ethical and moral aspects revolving around the technology. There are a number of ethical discussions revolving around other aspects such as mercy killing and abortions which are increasing the importance of the ethical aspects in any area.

However, there were a lot of developments in the field of applied ethics which is being used in the development of institutions, infrastructure, and technology which are the determining factors of survival in the society.

7.2. ETHICS FOR THE DIGITAL AGE: WHERE ARE THE MORAL SPECS?

The digital systems, institutions, infrastructures, and applications must be developed in accordance with the moral values so that the ethics play an important role in the digital world. The VSD perspective is an important aspect and is not restricted to technology development but is a part of different fields of engineering, medicine, science, and development.

The ethics is an important subject in recent times and if any technology that is not approved or does not meet the ethical standards would face difficulties in terms of approval, acceptance, and development. Therefore, the different technologies that are being developed in recent times keep in view the different ethical and moral constraints and are developed accordingly. The sudden shift in technology-centric world towards ethical aspects can be termed as "The Design Turn in Applied Ethics" (Van den Hoven et al., 2017).

7.2.1. Value Sensitive Design (VSD)

There were underpasses with low-level for the cars to pass and prevent buses from passing through, that were designed by a prominent architect called Robert Moses who was an urban planner. This was a main proposal to encourage private transport especially in the area of Jones Beach. This raised lot of social and political controversies as it prevented the poor and largely colored population to access the Jones Beach as they mostly traveled by public transport. This low-level underpass was criticized to act as borders between the wealthy and poor. The major assumption here is that technology is not unbiased with respect to values.

According to the VSD the process of development of technologies is as follows directly and systematically on the realization, or suppression, of particular configurations of social, ethical, and political values.

The idea and concept of the incorporation of social and moral values into the development of new technologies started in Stanford in the year 1970s, where ethics was the main subject of focus in the study of computer science. Where it was a central subject of study in Computer Science. This concept of value design later was incorporated into different areas and is called as the VSD.

VSD is a key area of research, and there are different research groups that are working in this area. The concept of VSD was initially suggest by Batya Friedman (2001) and followed by him there are a number of people who suggested different theories based on the concept of values and these theories are 'Values in Design' at University of California (Bowker; Gregory) at Irvine and NYU and 'Values for Design'.

There are a lot of methods or approaches for the values in design, and some of the important methods are as follows:

- The primary claim about the values in design is that there are different values that must be understood, analyzed, and incorporated into the existing and upcoming technologies.
- The process of understanding, analyzing, and the embedding of different ethical, moral, and value aspects into technology would pave way for the novel or future users to use the technology effectively.
- The secondary claim is that values and choices have a direct and tangible effects on those factors that are directly or indirectly involved.

Digital technologies are those that are present as computer interfaces, apps, menus, and webpages, search engines that give examples of selective architectures regarding how different people choose, act, and think. (Alina Huldtgren's overview, Design for values in IT) in Van den Hoven, Vermaas, and Van de Poel, Springer, 2015).

- The third claim is that the mindful and clear thought process regarding the values is more important to make morally correct inventions. Churchill stated before the House of Commons that: "first we shape our dwellings, and then our dwellings start to shape us."

The important fundamentals that design the lives of human beings and society are technology and innovation. There must be adequate thought that must be put into understanding the role of technology and the different impact on human beings in terms of technology.

- The important and final claim that is important for the value-design are the moral requirements that must be expressed in the initial stages of the procedure at the beginning of design and development would make a major difference to the value design.
- This approach is comparatively easy and gives rise to a theory called the "Colling ridge dilemma," and this theory postulates that "early in the process of development of a technology, the degrees of freedom for design are significant, but information that could inform design is relatively scarce, while later on in the development of the technology, as information starts to become available, the degrees of freedom in design have diminished."

7.2.2. Responsible Innovation

The innovations and creations team of Google called as the Google X has developed a novel product called as the Google Glass. The Google glass has voice-controlled access to internet and augmented reality features. The Google glass was taken for testing in the year 2014; however, there were a lot of privacy, safety, and security concerns, because of which the Google glass was stopped in the year 2015.

Google glass was discontinued because of the easily accessibility to take pictures via the Google lens which was not accepted by a number of people. The Google lens was an innovative project which gave the spectacles/ glasses a small camera to take pictures while checking out people. The easy access to data and the ability of the Google lens to take pictures of a everything people see, gave a number of security and privacy concerns because of which the project was discontinued. The Google glass was an innovative project that was started by Google; however, the major reason for the failure of this project was the ethical and moral considerations that Google failed to consider. However, Google lens is not the only innovative project that was withdrawn owing to the ethical and moral aspects. Netherlands is the other country which had to withdraw a whole project of smart electricity meters owing to the moral and ethical considerations.

Netherlands revolutionized and topped the aspect of digital innovation in the 21st century with the concept of the smart electricity meters across their country. There is need to make the electricity grids more efficient in every house in Netherlands to meet the targets of reduction of carbon dioxide (CO_2) from the environment by the year 2020.

The introduction of the smart electricity meters would have enabled Netherlands to top the digital network. The smart digital meters were made to analyze the electricity consumption in each household and understand the areas of high and low consumption. This would provide the citizens with the information regarding the different areas of electricity consumption and optimize their utilization, accordingly, and provide them with an opportunity to reduce their consumption and in turn minimize the electricity bill. The concept of smart meters was proposed in the parliament; however, the parliament did not approve the smart meter owing to the privacy and security constraints. This was another innovation which discontinued owing to privacy and security concerns was.

The meter is known as the 'spying device,' which would be harmful to the circle of individuals private life as it would take photographs/picture of the utilization of electricity almost every seven seconds and store the respective data in the database. This data would be utilized by the companies to understand the functioning of the homes of the individuals.

The important personal life data like the movies watched by the individuals at a time would also be known with little effort. The proposal was brought to the Dutch parliament, but it was rejected by the upper house for security and privacy of the citizens. The rejection of the smart meters in the parliament of Netherlands acted as a lesson to the other European countries as most of the other European countries that were planning to implement the concept of smart meters have withdrawn the idea of the smart meters.

There is a different example like the smart meter/ spying device in Netherland which is the introduction of electronic patient record system. The electronic patient record system took nearly ten years of research and development. However, after ten years of research, preparations, lobbying, stakeholder consultation and debates along with an investment of 300 million Euros the venture was banned in the parliament by the upper house because of privacy and security considerations. The novel ideas and innovations in the areas of electricity and health care sector would have enabled Netherlands to reduce the prices, improve their competence, become more sustainable with their objectives; however, the privacy and security concerns were the main reasons for hindrance in Netherlands for these aspects.

The health care sector would have seen major changes with respect to the maintenance of patient files and would have achieved better data security with respect to the patient data; however, the moral and ethical aspects have stopped the innovation in these areas.

These innovations would have been a huge revolutionary success if the engineers would have considered the moral and privacy aspects and combined these aspects into their innovations. The process of considering the moral and ethical aspects and giving them due importance while making an innovation is an important aspect of any innovation.

The major take-home point from these examples is that there is need to consider the moral and ethical values must be given importance as the "nonfunctional requirements," at an initial stage of the development of a project. The moral and ethical values are called as the nonfunctional requirements and the storage, capacity, speed, bandwidth, compliance with technical standards and protocols are called as the "functional requirements."

The smart meter and the electronic patient record system are undoubtedly the best innovative designs; however, any idea or design is considered to be a true innovation only if it has the capacity to fulfill all the requirements and enter into the market effectively. Both these projects failed because of lack of proper value sensitive thinking.

Value sensitive thinking is a process of understanding the different aspects of a design such as the efficiency, privacy, sustainability, and safety. A prior evaluation of all these factors and the impact of the innovation into the new market would save a lot of time, energy, and resources. If the engineers have carefully analyzed and understood these aspects, they should have integrated them into their innovations which would have made these innovations a great success.

The smart meter is not made available because of privacy and security concerns, but it can be redesigned by installing privacy and security features. There is a lot of debate and several oppositions regarding the redesigning of the smart meter, among which the initial one is regarding the moralism and the second one is regarding the relativism.

The major debate is regarding the values that must be inbuilt, whether there is need for the values to be inbuilt and the reason for the values to be inbuilt. There are a lot of different types of values; however, the values provided by the pragmatic research methods are not coherent and steady. The objections related to moralism and relativism can be easily addressed as technology is never neutral (Van den Hoven, 2013) and a technology, application or service can be preferred by the expense of another though it was either planned or unplanned.

The process of the consideration of different values (ethical and moral) in the development of technologies is an important element, and there are a variety of technologies that are being developed based on the values. The process of VSD followed by responsible innovation is an important strategy that is adapted in the development of new technologies.

The theories of moralism and relativism are the important theories that are affecting the development of various technologies. These theories and the other aspects of technology play an important in the research and development stage that revolves around the development of various novel technologies.

The example of 'privacy enhancing technologies' can be taken into consideration by focusing on the protection of data and ensuring the privacy has been asked from the European Union by ensuring privacy and security.

The whole world is concentrating on the development of cyber technologies with better data security and is known to be privacy enhancing, and these technologies with better data security and privacy are called as the privacy enhancing technologies and these privacy enhancing technologies are widely used by incorporating different ethical and moral considerations.

The data is a central aspect of the whole world, and the raising of big data and data analytics is enabling the users to utilize products and service across the world by valuing the user requirements and ethical values like privacy, security, and identity. There are a lot of countries that are using the data science and analytics, and over most of them especially Europe is having an advantage to be a crucial commercial player in the field of IT.

There is need for more innovation as that would enable to provide with answers to the circumstances with moral overload (Van den Hoven et al., 2012). There is one circumstance where there is moral overload and the other circumstance where there is burden of the contradictory responsibilities and values that are needed to be known simultaneously. There is need for genuine privacy and national security which can be achieved by proper utilization of technology and innovation.

The differences in economic growth and technology were solved by the utilization of sustainable technology. The answers to these problems are known to be the 'technical fixes' and are not interpreted as frank solutions to some of those moral overloads/problems. These situations need no opinion and need to be tackled to bring about a difference by design or innovation.

The fundamental aspect that is functional is as follows:

"If a contingent state of the world at time t1 does not allow us to satisfy two or more of our moral values or moral obligations at the same time, they did not bring about change by innovation in the world at t1 that allows us to satisfy them all together at a later time t2, then there is need have a moral obligation at t1 to innovate" (Van den Hoven, 2013).

The major aspect of any innovation or novel product is the accountability to that innovation. The moral and ethical aspects are the major aspects that are accountable in the process of designing any novel idea or making any innovation. The process of being accountable to any innovation and making the necessary changes in the product to make the innovation a success, demonstrate the sense of responsibility to that innovation.

There are many aspects that need to be considered while making any innovation and the important aspects are:

- The privacy and security of an innovation;
- The moral and ethical aspects that revolve around an innovation;
- The financial aspect of the innovation;
- The sustainability of that innovative idea;
- The safety and security of a particular innovation.

The fundamental rule normally is that the 'ought' to would mean 'can' it hold, and a notable aspect is that the secondary aspect is that it does not mean 'can.'

This refers to the fact that there is a need to be responsible to create novel technologies to resolve few problems without any assured success. There is a need for an advanced level of moral obligation that would bring about a difference in the thought process of how we innovate.

There is a necessity to understand and learn about the various ethical and moral values that are needed in the research and development at the initial stages. There is need to understand the functional and operational aspects of the values as they are 'functionally decomposed' and there is need to comprehend the minor and major specifications in the engineering and design work. Responsible innovation is an important concept of the different technologies that are developed according to the moral and ethical considerations. The different stages and important aspects of responsible innovation are as follows:

- The information and knowledge must be obtained from the different sources carefully before taking them for analysis.
- The different outcomes and the existing options must be effectively analyzed and executed.
- The above two points the need to obtain and to evaluate recommend that there is one more inference which is called as the Responsible Innovation which can have the moral agents that are related.
- These two aspects must be considered and used in the process of designing new technologies and products based on the moral aspects.

The responsible innovation can be categorized based on the need for innovation and its related events in the given manner: responsible innovation is a novel process which involves around the different aspects and designs that are revolving around the following aspects that are related to the:

- Physical world which involves the planning and development of different buildings and infrastructure.
- Conceptual world which relates to the development of different concepts pertaining to the different concepts and theories pertaining to mathematics, science, and other areas of computer science.
- Institutional world which revolves around the implementation of different social and legal aspects pertaining to the different institutions and organizations.

Sometimes responsible innovation is revolving around these worlds independently and many numbers of times these are revolving around different aspects that are a combination of one or more elements from these worlds.

7.3. AUTONOMOUS AGENTS

7.3.1. Characteristics of Autonomous Agents

There are two major aspects in the field of Autonomous Intelligence called as the 'Strong' and 'weak.' The strong in autonomous intelligence refers to the development of technologies which are better than human intelligence and can-do aspects better than human beings, whereas the weak refers to the beings with limited capabilities which are not better than human intelligence in any way. The examples of weak autonomous intelligent agents are computer vision systems, game-playing software, and others.

There are a lot of debates on the strong vs. weak concept, but the importance of all of them is the philosophical debate regarding which of them is better. However, the important of all the autonomous intelligent agents is that they are not part of the strong autonomous intelligence but are mostly these are technologies and applications that imitate natural intelligence.

The autonomous agents are designed to extremely smart and have a very high intellect, and they can be either in the form of software or this software that are integrated into a physical system called as the robots. The major change in the operation of the softbots and the software is dependent on the type of surroundings that these softbots must function. The environment in which these softbots interact, and function is called as the cyberspace. Softbots are capable of communicating to the human beings from their virtual world, and they are interesting aspects of technology.

The software autonomous agents and the softbots/robots do not have many differences when compared to one another. The important aspect of any softbot or robot is that they have an inbuilt software system which is called as the firmware which would enable the robot function according to the designed capabilities.

The complete understanding of the autonomous agents gives us a comprehension that these are predesigned software programs. Autonomous agents are unique in their own way, as every computer program is designed and programmed differently, therefore each autonomous agent is different. The difference between each autonomous agent make them unique, and these autonomous agents are independent in their own way.

Autonomous agents have a wide range of applications because of their uniqueness and independent functioning; as a result, they are widely used in cyberwarfare. The autonomous agents have been defined differently by a number of people; however, Franklin and Graesser gave the most standard definition for the autonomous agents, which is as follows "An autonomous agent is a system situated within and a part of an environment that senses that environment and acts on it, over time, in pursuit of its own agenda and to effect what it senses in the future."

The major aspects regarding the autonomous agents which are part of this definition are as follows (Figure 7.1):

- The autonomous intelligent agent is completely and stringently related to the surroundings.
- The autonomous agent that is present away from the respective surroundings is known to have no use or function, or it is not considered to be an autonomous agent.
- There are proper sensors that are used to communicate with the surroundings.
- There are proper actuators along with the sensors that are used to interact with surroundings and are known to function in a way that can create some impact on their surroundings.
- The autonomous agent's function with a defined motto or aim which is called as 'agenda' by the Franklin and Graesser.
- The autonomous agents that are made to be used in the warfare are called as the targets.
- The functions of a completely autonomous agent are established over a period so that they have a sustainability related to an assigned function.
- There is certain feature of an autonomous agent that are not mentioned here; however, they can be understood and comprehended from the knowledge that is gained from the aspects mentioned here.

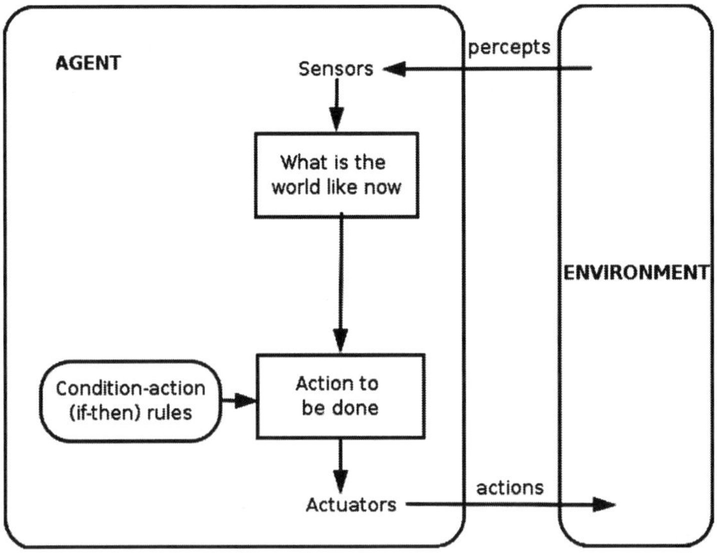

Figure 7.1: Autonomous agents.

Source: https://upload.wikimedia.org/wikipedia/commons/3/3f/IntelligentAgent-SimpleReflex.png

The important elements regarding the autonomous agents are as follows:

The main aspect of these independent agents is that they should have inner surroundings that represent their functioning which is called as the "belief state." Based on their internal surroundings these autonomous agents are classified into different types by Stuart Russell and Peter Norvig in their reference book for artificial intelligence (AI). The classification is based on the environment of these robots, based on which these autonomous agents are classified into following types. They are:

- Simple reflex dependent autonomous agents- these are not dependent on the inner environment;
- Model dependent autonomous agents;
- Goal dependent autonomous agents;
- Utility dependent autonomous agents.

The agents that are based on the function and utilization are known to the illustrations of their internal surroundings that would act as the precursors to guess the actions of the agents and the measure of the utility like the platform to outlet the different states of the environment.

The utility function is the most important aspect of the autonomous agents, and the utility function is the fundamental aspect used by Russell and Norvig's when they used the term "rational" in defining the autonomous agent.

An autonomous agent is called rational when it can act or select a function based on the surrounding and the internal knowledge that is used to perform a function.

The given process is a summary to the whole procedure where there is a pressure on an autonomous agent to be completely intelligent and the given inner information about the utilization of an autonomous agent must change over a certain period. There is a need for the autonomous agent to learn from its experiences and store the knowledge gained from each experience. These changes could be in the form of adjustments in each goal and the respective target and may have the related strong implications in the field of cyber offense.

There are few more concepts in addition to the given concepts so that the autonomous agents are truly intelligent. They are given below:

- Autonomous agents should be independent and have a prototype of the inner surroundings in which they can function.
- Autonomous agents must have their own goal, which is required for the autonomous agent to determine its function or utility based on the goal.
- Autonomous agent must have the ability to understand and learn new aspects.
- Autonomous agents need to be easily adaptable, as they should change themselves according to the internal environment.

7.3.2. Taxonomy Related to Autonomous Agents

Taxonomy of the autonomous agents refers to classification of the autonomous agents. The different autonomous agents that are described previously are the robotic and computational agents. These are further classified into different types.

The computational agents are further classified based on divided into two broad categories based on the different aspects such as the policies, strategies, and the different cyber operational doctrines that must be integrated into these agents. These autonomous agents are further classified into two types based on their role such as:

- Autonomous agents that are used to acquire knowledge; and
- Autonomous agents that are used in military operations.

The autonomous agents that are utilized to acquire knowledge are not dangerous, whereas the autonomous agents that are used in different military operations are known to be damaging in nature as they can identify the target and act accordingly.

The autonomous agents are categorized into two types based on their architecture. They are:

- Monolithic Agents; and
- Decentralized Agents.

Monolithic agents: Monolithic agents are those autonomous agents that are made from one source of information and the functionalities of the monolithic agents are limited. For example, monolithic agents are any date file or software libraries that have different information.

Decentralized agents or Decentralized Intelligent Agents: Decentralized agents are called as decentralized intelligent agents and as per their name they refer to the systems where the intelligence is distributed among many different elements. Though the intelligence is distributed these elements function in coordination with one another and are called as the "artificial flocks" by Craig Reynolds because of the demonstrated similarities in the way they live or function.

The decentralized agent is known to more resistant to the efforts related to deactivating and the impacts of counteroffensives. Therefore, for an example, a botnet is a network of various agents in the place of the conventional malware software which would be the central point of control that would be deactivated.

The important aspect that needs to be considered is that the independent agents that are used in cyberwarfare are not known and there is no information that is officially available regarding the different autonomous agents that are used in the cyberwarfare. The limited knowledge and information that is available regarding the artificial autonomous agents do not describe the complete information regarding the agents that are used in the cyberwarfare.

The important theories of the computational autonomous agents are:

- The autonomous agents do not represent the surroundings in which they function.
- The autonomous agents are not efficient in acquiring new information.

- The autonomous agents are not capable of assessing a target, choosing an action and functioning accordingly.
- The autonomous agents are not capable of functioning according to time, and they do not indicate a flow or continuity of time.
- The autonomous agents are not capable of making independent choices; however, they choose their targets and functions based on a set of guidelines that were used to program these agents.

7.3.3. The Environment of Softbots

The physical autonomous agents are called as robots, and they work in the regular physical environment where there are a lot of computational agents, and this environment is called as cyberspace.

The cyberspace has various definitions and the white house cyberspace policy review which was published in the year 2011 defines the cyberspace as "the interdependent network of IT infrastructures, and includes the Internet, telecommunications networks, computer systems and embedded processors and controllers in critical industries."

Cyberspace is a different and specific environment that is created by human beings and hence it's very exclusive. The cyberspace is made, preserved, and used by a number of people from different private and public sectors, the diversity of the audience would need the cyberspace to be dynamic.

The cyberspace and its surroundings have different characteristics, and according to the Russell and Norvig's classification the different peculiarities of cyberspace are listed as follows:

- Cyberspace does not have completely available surroundings.
- The different aspects of cyberspace are not available at the same time.
- Any person at a given time would have knowledge of only one small aspect of cyberspace.
- The cyberspace is a very intricate and difficult environment.
- Cyberspace is very dynamic, diverse, and unique space as it is constantly changing with respect to its utility and different requirements.
- Cyberspace is the area which is prone to different sort of warfare and sometimes highly susceptible, despite the presence of

cybersecurity software like the firewalls, Intrusion Detection Systems (IDSs) and Intrusion Prevention Systems (IPSs).

7.4. ETHICS OF VIRTUAL AUTONOMY

We now turn to the particular ways in which issues of autonomy and agency play out in our five selected technologies (Figure 7.2).

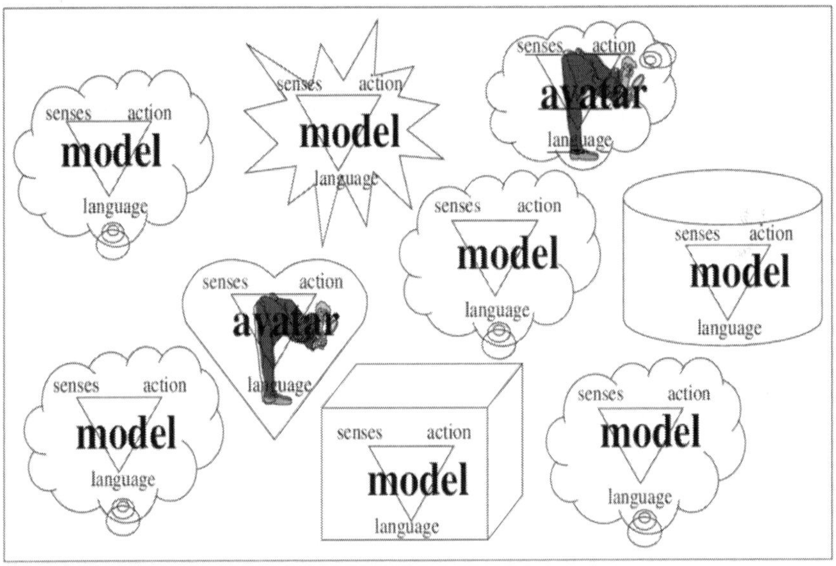

Figure 7.2: Autonomy and virtual reality.

Source: https://www.researchgate.net/figure/Autonomy-and-Virtual-Reality_fig5_239550135

7.4.1. ALife

At the time of 1960s, the exponential development of speed as well as the capacity of storage within the integrated circuits was identified, providing others with what is now commonly known as Moore's Law (Moore, 1965).

Partially this is because of the fact that ALife researchers have initiated with what researchers already had an idea of, in hindsight to be extremely simplistic perceptions regarding the connection between genotypes and phenotypes. Till the process of the development of organisms is entirely understood, ALife 'organisms' will certainly be present but caricatures belonging to the actual living entities. Though there persists plenty, which is artificial regarding the ALife, however, still not much has been provide that is considerably life-like about it.

The restrictions or the limitations associated with the technology have been prominent here for both the virtual as well as the physically embodied ALife is required to, therefore, temper concerns relating to ALife, somehow fleeing the grasps of the existing scientists, and running berserk.

7.4.2. Embodied Artificial Agents

Embodied artificial agents have been structured or designed for the purpose of operation within physical environments. Cyborgs have been considered as one of the main genera belonging to the embodied artificial agents, the other major genus being the robots that are entirely inorganic in their respective nature.

In the end, Pistorius has not been victorious in beating the qualifying time for entrance to the 400 m event, though his specified time surely would be putting him well beyond the average running speed of human beings. Perhaps, the definition of dictionary generally tends to exclude Oscar Pistorius from the category related to cyborgs on the grounds, which is Cheetah blades that was supposed to get strapped on, not 'built into' the provided body.

Setting up with the definitional matters separately, the types of cyborgs that possess most of the interest for the purposes of this chapter are usually those which provides with an offer regarding the cognitive enhancements to the humans with the help of embed computational devices.

The 'cyborg divide' could be only as considerate if all these improvements provide with core keys to those who tend to adopt them. Specified advancements also raise certain issues related to ethics.

7.4.3. Virtual Artificial Agents

Virtual artificial agents (aka 'bots') are already into existence. They operate inside computationally generated environments. The range of a general virtual artificial agent starts with internet as whole till the electronic market. The electronic market is generally referred to the e-commerce market which has started gaining momentum at a global level. Some of the famous examples for electronic markets are; NASDAQ and eBay. The range of virtual artificial agent from electronic market gets extended to computer games, and they exist within networked virtual worlds such as Second Life that are designed primarily for entertainment, but are also increasingly being used for communication and education.

In the electronic markets, there persists automated trading along with the bidding programs, which helps in carrying out all the transactions that are entirely based on the provided formulas that in some cases are a far from the comprehension of those who tend to depend or rely upon them.

The fact that most of the people possess the tendency to overestimate the intellectuality along with the criticality of computer programs, which is now known to the AI researchers in the form of 'ELIZA effect.' It is just a demonstration of the formerly mentioned tendency of human beings to anthropomorphize the pertaining things.

The perspective for 'persuasion' by non-verbal means is just the starting to get probed, but the probable for ethical abuse in situations like these is already quite tacit.

7.4.4. Machine-Centered VR

The general example of online auctions helps in illustrating this. Due to the format within which information has been provided favors regarding the machines, they possess much more capability or potentiality in comparison to those of the human beings of precisely timing an ultimate proffer to be victorious in an auction at the last second level.

The issues related to ethics that are being raised by VR environments which are machine- centered, are thus, not only regarding the artificial agents, who are functioning within them, but impose a concern on the limitations that have been placed by such environments upon people who try to work within them.

7.4.5. Anthropomorphic VR

Anthropomorphic VR has been deployed for many purposes, including games, cybersex, teleconferencing, pilot training, soldier training, elementary school education, and it is under investigation for use in many more applications, for instance, police lineups. Such applications make distinct demands, based on the amount of realism that has been involved within it. Flight imitators, for example, objects to be realistic in almost all facets.

Whenever the person is functioning being the single user within a remote VR application, the issues belonging to the ethics have been raised by the pertaining actions within that specific environment are essentially indirect.

Thus, opportunities like these are not being considered as ethically neutral, however.

They might be having an impact on the other individuals directly, or possess indirect effects by the process of training or strengthening the habits of action that might be spilling over into the actual world.

7.5. CYBERATTACK SCENARIOS FOR AUTONOMOUS AGENTS

Cyberwarfare is the important term of recent times as there is a lot of research, discussions, and arguments that are being carried out in the recent times. The majority of the speculation and debates about the cyberwarfare in the recent times is mostly focused on the defense from the attack and the important reasons for this are:

- Secrecy that is maintained in the different software and applications;
- A variety of political aspects and stakeholders that are involved in these cyber attacks;
- The accessibility to information;
- The privacy settings that are maintained by different organizations regarding the data.

The concept of cyberwarfare is mostly focusing on the defense rather than the attack. There is need to understand the different stages of cyberwarfare to prepare well for the cyberwarfare. The proper understanding of the different stages of the cyber-attack would enable the organizations to prepare well for the cyber-attack and strategize the defense strategy accordingly (Figure 7.3).

Figure 7.3: Cyberattack.

Source:https://cdn.pixabay.com/photo/2018/04/17/11/02/cyber–3327240_960_720.jpg

7.5.1. Reconnaissance

Reconnaissance is an important aspect of any cyber-attack as the reconnaissance refers to that stage of cyber-attack which involves research, identification, and selection of the target.

Reconnaissance is the start to most belligerent processes and is called as the initial stage of a cyber-attack as it offers a perfect environment for the disposition of autonomous agents. The disposition of agents happens in three directions. They are:

- Automatic discovery of technical vulnerabilities in target systems or networks;
- The process of collecting information about the technical vulnerabilities like the specifications of the assembly and topology of different operating systems and applications; and
- The process of acquiring information about different users, and different personal security credentials of the users that would give an access to the cyberattacks.

The process of identification of the weakness and the possible susceptibilities in the target network to strategize the attack is an important stage of planning a cyber-attack. The cyber-attacks are researched, planned, and executed by skilled professionals who are pioneers in the areas of cyber-attack.

The software autonomous agent is known to reconnoiter the target, identify, and differentiate the susceptibilities and strategizes a method to exploit these susceptibilities. Although complete automation of exploit development is not extensively accessible, there are some scenarios that are utilized for the incorporation of agents with that competence.

The important stages of the cyber-attack are as follows:

- **Reconnaissance:** Reconnaissance involves the process of researching about the objects, identification of the objects and selection of the targets.
- **Weaponization:** The process of the weaponization involves the combination of the different malware to the researched targets.
- **Delivery:** The process of delivering or sending the malware or viruses to the identified and selected targets by the emails, messages, pen drives, different attachments, and other routes.
- **Exploitation:** The delivered viruses or malware start becoming sensitive and execute the harmful set of operations that are programmed in the malware.
- **Installation:** The process of exploitation becomes effective with the successful installation of the harmful malware which would give them access to the data of the target continuously.
- **Command and Control:** The installed malware not just provides the existing information, but also gives access to the users which would enable outsiders to establish a command on the system and control the targets activities.
- **Actions on objective:** The attackers would plan and execute the attack with a set of objectives which are successfully achieved with the attack. These objectives would vary according to the requirements of the attackers, and they could be things like destruct the data, access the data or replace the data, gain control over the network or corrupt a software and any more.

The process of planning, executing, and achieving the desired result by a cyber-attack would create a damage that could not be measured by magnitude. The whole process of cyber-attack and its damage cannot be measured; therefore, an important strategy could be defending and design defensive strategies into the network rather than being susceptible technologies. There are different types of protections that can ensure data privacy and security in the network.

- The autonomous agents or the software agents are mostly given training or a set of instructions to attack a particular network.
- The next stage would be the process of acquiring information that is needed to target a network.
- Beyond the information gathering stage is the stage of infiltration, wherein the different autonomous agents would attack a network based on a set of instructions that were programmed into the agent prior to the attack.
- The decentralized agents are executed to plan a perfect attack where the same action is divided into different set of packets and each agent is programmed differently to execute the attack.
- The fundamental motto of this type of action is the collection of data that would be directed to the command and control structure for further processing. The different technical and other information regarding the susceptibilities is gathered, and this information is used to execute the attack (Figure 7.4).

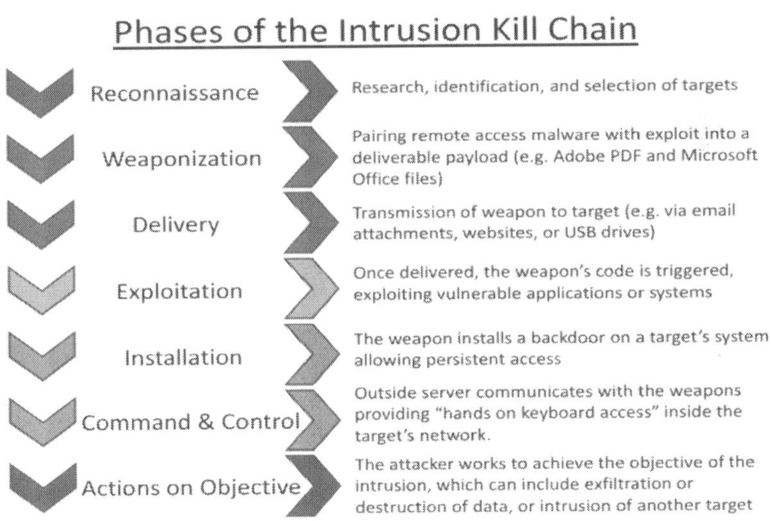

Figure 7.4: Stages of cyberattack.

Source: https://upload.wikimedia.org/wikipedia/commons/thumb/1/1d/Intrusion_Kill_Chain_-_v2.png/800px-Intrusion_Kill_Chain_-_v2.png

7.5.2. Infiltration and Beyond

The autonomous agents are used to gather or acquire information, and these agents are used to remember the data that is acquired during the whole process of reconnaissance and this information which consists of different vulnerabilities is used to plan an attack. This process is called as the infiltration. The major strategy that is used to plan an attack or infiltration is by the method of using "trees."

Trees are the different structures that are used in signifying certain problems in AI. These trees in artificial agents are used to design different strategies in the process of the cyber-attack. These trees are used as models for the future attacks that are planned. These trees act as representatives to plan the future acts of infiltration and successfully execute the present process of infiltration. The process of representation of the inner surrounding and the different vulnerabilities would enable the autonomous agents to protect and combat against the defenders. This process would make the autonomous agents more "persistent" and such threats to these autonomous agents are called as the "advanced persistent threats" (APTs).

The proper knowledge and representation of the possible threats would make the autonomous agents understand the appropriate defensive strategies and enable them to prepare themselves accordingly and be successful in executing the attack.

The intelligent autonomous agents would acquire information, understand the possible countermeasures and act accordingly. The whole process of understanding different strategies and preparing against these strategies and being counteractive would enable the autonomous agents to be stronger and use different techniques of AI to protect the information and successfully carry forward their objective.

7.5.3. Swarms

Swarms are called as the decentralized agents that are independently programmed and can execute different sets of commands. These decentralized agents though have distributed functions and diverse roles they are called "artificial flocks" and can communicate amongst each other to execute a task effectively. The network that is formed by a set of decentralized agents is very strong and is extremely difficult to combat, and they should be handled both independently and collectively to protect a system against a set of decentralized agents.

7.5.4. Command and Control

The process of cyberwarfare or cyber-attack begins with prior research, identification of the target, infiltration, and followed by the process of acquiring command and control on the data and information of the target. There are a lot of factors that determine and are instrumental in acquiring the command and control over the cyberwarfare such as the identified potential vulnerabilities and the design of the programs accordingly. There are a set of preprogrammed instructions in the malware which play an important role in attacking the target and gaining access over the target database.

The process of acquiring command and control over the target database is a major security breach as it can cause serious privacy and security threats. If the target is the army database or any financial database, then the loss that is caused by the attack of this malware cannot be measured.

These attacks must be expected, and the security settings of the software must be updated in order to protect from these malicious attacks, and there are a set of tactics, techniques, and procedures that are used for the intelligent autonomous agents to protect them from the malicious cyber-attacks.

7.6. THE LEGAL LANDSCAPE

The cyber-attacks are having serious implications, and there are an increasing number of discussions in legal platform regarding the implementation of the international law to the cyberwarfare. There are several serious consequences and the development in the fields of computers and technology are increasing, and the increase in the use of technology is increasing the vulnerabilities and making the technology prone to attack.

There are a number of laws that are developing to regulate these attacks and increase the punishment for the people who are involved in designing and executing the attacks. There are several cyber laws that are being enforced, and the important laws are discussed.

The international body of law that is governing the cyberwarfare is basically consisting of two bodies, and they are:

- *Jus as bellum*; and
- *Jus in bello.*

Jus as bellum is the international law that governs the resort to force by the states and the Jus in bello which is called as the international humanitarian law is mostly involve in the governing of the various armed conflicts and implementation of the law of neutrality.

7.6.1. Jus Ad Bellum

The foremost foundation of the international *jus ad bellum* is the Charter of the United Nations that was signed in San Francisco in the year 1945, and its consecutive modifications. Article 2(4) of the Charter concerns the use of force by Members: "All Members shall refrain in their international relations from the threat or use of force against the territorial integrity or political independence of any state."

According to the charter, the cyberwarfare is defined as something which has effects "comparable to those likely to result from kinetic, chemical, biological or nuclear weapons," and in this regard, self-sufficient agents are similar to the other tools that are used in cyberwarfare.

7.6.2. Jus in Bello (International Humanitarian Law)

Jus in Bello is called as the international humanitarian law. This law is used to govern the activities related to armed forces and warfare. The main foundations of this law are derived from the Geneva conventions from the year 1949, and there are certain additional protocols which are from the year 1977, and there are certain aspects adapted from a much earlier Hague Convention which was done in the year 1907.

7.7. CONCLUSION

Autonomous technologies are those technologies that are independent and are developed based on certain principles of the computer science and engineering. The autonomous technologies can be either simple computer software or softbots that have a set of programmed instructions and software incorporated into them.

The technology development was mostly technocentric in the early seventies and eighties, as a result of which the earlier days' technologies were more focused on the concept and technology, whereas in the new times especially in the twenty-first-century ethics is an important element of computer science. The ethics and morals are a set of values that determine the process of development of novel technology. The importance to ethics is developing in the recent times, and the importance to ethical values is being largely debated not just in the field of computer science but in the fields of science, medicine, and technology. The important elements from other fields that are being largely debated based on the ethical concepts are the mercy killing and abortions.

Values are an integral part of any technology, and the values can be either ethical values or moral values. Therefore, several technologies in recent times were using a VSD, and there is a need to incorporate these aspects into technologies, as otherwise, these technologies may fail to come into existence. The Google glass, smart meters, and automated patient record systems are the examples of failure of great and innovative technologies that ceased to exist because of social and ethical issues.

Responsible innovation is the other aspect of the technology development as there is need to be responsible in creation, as a simple lack of responsibility in designing a new technology would lead to a failure in the development of technology.

Autonomous agents are classified into different types based on their function, topology, and architecture. The important categories of the autonomous agents are the monolithic agents and decentralized agents. Monolithic agents are single pieces of software such as the data files, whereas the decentralized agents involve the division of power among different smaller agents which function collectively.

The important risk to the autonomous agents is the cyberwarfare, and the cyberwarfare is a preplanned and executed attack to get access to the data and information. There are different stages of the cyber-attack, and they are Reconnaissance, Weaponization, Delivery, Exploitation, Installation, Command, and Control, Actions on the objective which result in a data breach and lead to different security concerns.

The cyberwarfare is generally, and it is difficult to stop a security attack; instead, most of the methods that involve the protection from cyber-attacks are defense strategies. There is importance that needs to be given to installing strong firmware and protect the agents from data breach and security concerns.

Data is an important aspect of computer science, and there must be due importance that must be given to the ethical and privacy aspects of data privacy and security. The study of computer ethics is extremely important, and there is a need to understand the various aspects of ethics and moral aspects that need to be considered and incorporated into technologies to develop successful technologies.

REFERENCES

1. Center, L., (n.d.). [online] Available at: https://www.lorentzcenter.nl/lc/web/2016/852/description.php3? wsid¼852&venue¼Oort [Accessed 13 Nov. 2018].
2. Friedman, B., Hendry, G. D., Huldtgren, A., & Van Wynsberghe, A., (2018). [online] Available at: https://www.researchgate.net/publication/283435670_Charting_the_Next_Decade_for_Value_Sensitive_Design [Accessed 13 Nov. 2018].
3. Podins, K., Stinissen, J., & Maybaum, M., (2013). *5th International Conference on Cyberconflict*. [online] Ccdcoe.org. Available at: https://ccdcoe.org/cycon/2013/proceedings/cyconBOOK2013.pdf [Accessed 13 Nov. 2018].
4. Van Den Hoven, J., (2017). *Ethics for the Digital Age: Where Are the Moral Specs?* [online] Available at: https://link.springer.com/content/pdf/10.1007%2F978–3–319–55735–9_6.pdf[Accessed 13 Nov. 2018].
5. E. Moore, G. (1965). Cramming more components onto integrated circuits. [ebook] Available at: http://www.monolithic3d.com/uploads/6/0/5/5/6055488/gordon_moore_1965_article.pdf [Accessed 17 Mar. 2019].
6. Van den Hoven, J., Lokhorst, G. and Van de Poel, I. (2012). Engineering and the Problem of Moral Overload. *Science and Engineering Ethics*, 18(1), pp.143-155.
7. van den Hoven, J. (2013). Value Sensitive Design and Responsible Innovation. Responsible Innovation, pp.75-83.
8. Janssen, M. and van den Hoven, J. (2015). Big and Open Linked Data (BOLD) in government: A challenge to transparency and privacy?. Government Information Quarterly, 32(4), pp.363-368.
9. Borning, A., Friedman, B. and H. Kahn, Jr., P. (2001). *Value Sensitive Design: Theory and Methods*. [ebook] Available at: https://faculty.washington.edu/pkahn/articles/vsd-theory-methods-tr.pdf [Accessed 17 Mar. 2019].
10. Thaler, R., Sunstein, C. and Balz, J. (2010). Choice Architecture. *SSRN Electronic Journal*.
11. Clark, A. and Chalmers, D. (1998). The Extended Mind. Analysis, 58(1), pp.7-19.

8

Regulatory Issues and Challenges

CONTENTS

Computer security is a topic of concern in the field of computer ethics. Everybody is living in the era of computer viruses and international spying by hackers. The problem is not only with the physical security of the hardware like protecting it from theft, fire, flood, etc. but also with the logical security like privacy and confidentially. Malicious kinds of software, or "programmed threats," provide a significant challenge to computer security. Computer crimes, such as embezzlement or planting of logic bombs, are normally committed by trusted personnel who have permission to use the computer system. Computer security, therefore, must also be concerned with the actions of trusted computer users. Computer professionals are ready for the challenges that are coming in the form of new technology. One of the more controversial areas of computer ethics concerns the intellectual property rights connected with software ownership.

8.1. INTRODUCTION

Ethics is a way of thinking positively or negatively which can also be applied professionally as well as personally in a day-to-day life. People want to do things in a right way so that they show some kind of profession. Ethics may be defined in different ways. It is the codes of morals of a particular profession, or it is an agreement among people to covert the wrong things in a right way.

Computer Ethics can be defined as allowing the individual to find solutions for the problems and the individual should work in a right way. The biggest challenge for the individuals is to handle the tough situations and make it simple and clean to work in a right way.

The technology has been changing day-to-day which are making the impact on the people's life. The major issues which are faced by the individuals, as well as the organizations, is that they are not updated with the new technology and later they are facing some kind of ethical problems. For example, the issue of a company officially monitoring employees' e-mail is very controversial issues.

It is necessary for the individuals to understand the computer ethics. Nowadays, computers have become the need for every individual along with the lot of challenges. There are many computer users who have less knowledge and find difficult to overcome the situations. The individuals are faced by several challenges, and they face trouble to express their views in an electronic mail. It is necessary to understand computer ethics related to privacy issues and security. It is also important to understand major negative impacts of IT with the help of advanced computer technology. The difference between what is illegal and what is unethical is not always obvious. It has no surprise that IT sector and IT society can also become negative which will have an impact on the education, social skills, privacy, and security.

There is a need for technology in each sector so the term "computer ethics" is required to analyze that what is wrong and right for internet users. It is necessary to find that the information technology (IT) is affecting the society or not.

According to the experts, there has been provided lot of security in the IT sector. It is necessary to keep the information in a private and followed by the major projection. Experts believe that it should not make the negative impacts of IT on cyberspace.

The approach should be technical if the individual is working on the digital ID methods, encryption, and firewall. These approaches have been followed to find the solutions of the problems, and legal actions can also be taken to find the increasing number of ethical problems.

Computer Ethics should be concern for everyone because the information, data, and computer networks can be exposed by many internal and external hazards internationally. Every country has its own Government so all the computer professionals, public policy makers, organizations, and private citizens should take an interest and make their contributions for the development of the country. This global information can be broken in a socially and ethically sensitive way for everyone's future benefit and applications.

8.2. ETHICAL CHALLENGES ON INFORMATION TECHNOLOGY

Many of them are facing some serious ethical challenges, but the users and IT Experts mainly who are working in the IT department are ready to face the biggest challenges. At times, most of the users and IT experts do not know that how to go about the challenges as more emerging and evolving information technologies are pop up on the market.

The major issue which affecting the society are lack of security, privacy, copyright violation. The main challenge which is faced in the IT sector are increasing in the number of crimes in the IT sector. Every individual wants to use internet in a different way, but they make a mistake of misusing the computers which can result in making a crime.

Many organizations, as well as successful businesses, are afraid of losing their information or data because of hackers who can easily hack and use the company's information for their own benefits. There should be more privacy to control the information.

There are some issues with the employees also as they are not faithful and can use IT to archive their personal goals which might be risky and harmful to an organization. IT is not taken as bad by its self, but the way humans use the tools provided by IT for their own benefit has brought some serious challenges.

8.2.1. Security

Nowadays, many organizations are facing this issue for a long time that the hackers found it very easy to hack the system or computer with tools that are like connected to the internet. Internet Protocol is a number assigned to any machine that has a computer network, and that uses the internet protocol for communicating, and this protocol can easily be used by the hackers for addressing to access a user's computer and collect data for selfish reasons. Most of the organization believes that the hacker will collect data for their own benefit.

The widespread of internet cookies which collect information whenever the internet is used has exposed IT users to high risks of fraud and conflicting interests.

There are lots of companies who are specialized in IT field, and they have the strategy to use the cookies so that can get control over their products or services. The customers also face trouble at the time of transferring their money to another account because of hackers as they can do fraud to the bank and the customers and transfer money to their own account which is quite illegal.

8.2.2. Copyright Infringement

All kind of information is available on the internet, and users use that information in their work which is not allowed. The users are allowed to take the idea from the concept and not to misuse the information in their work life. For example, many music companies and photo bookmarking sites are facing the difficulty because of the people who are unnecessary using the information and sharing them. As a result, the original makers are suffering from loss, and they are not getting the benefit of their work.

The one who has created music albums may suffer a loss as the songs or music is being downloaded as free over the internet. Lots of original work like music albums, books, and file downloading sites are popping up on internet every day. In this case, one real user will purchase the book, web template, software or music album, and they will submit it to a free download site where others will simply just download that data for free.

The government plan has come into action because it has banned some of the sites like MEGAUPLOAD.COM because many users are misusing it which will affecting the work of original makers. It is giving benefit to the users, but it is not allowed.

8.2.3. Increased Computer Crimes

The person can do fraud in order to make money. This becomes biggest challenge for the IT experts' team to take care of the systems and check every day and protect from the hackers. Many users who have the knowledge and skills to use the systems should have the availability for making a crime. For example, many organizations have developed the strategy and made a strong IT team who are ready to control these issues in any manner and solve the queries within a day.

8.2.4. Digital Divide

The growth and development of the countries are mainly depending on the IT sector. More progress will be there if more improvement in the IT sector. Many developing counties are lacking in some areas to update the users with new technology. Government knows that there has been a lack of technology in some areas and people want to adopt the new culture. It has been taking a time to develop the areas, as the technology sector also seems to be very costly for the government.

But the problem is faced by small areas of the country because they do not have enough power to use IT tools like computer. In other sectors related to education, most of these developing countries have poor old education systems, so a student will not be aware of new information technologies.

8.3. ETHICAL ISSUES IN INFORMATION TECHNOLOGY

The business and organization will be more successful only with the high level of technology. For Example, goods, and services can be exchanged or moved with the relevant information can give profit to the business.

Nowadays, Information is necessary to move the business ahead, and IT play a major role in the business, and there can be also sharing of data with the help of software, telecommunication, computer hardware and digital electronics for making the business successful.

According to the experts, ethical attentions for Information and Communications Technology associated issues first looked under the topic "information ethics (IE)" in the Annual Review of Information Science and Technology in 1992. This advises that there is an ethical program related with the use of Information and Communications Technology. Organizations and Individuals then need to be ethically delicate as they organize ICT on their actions and procedures.

The impact of Information and Communications Technology on human relationship has been tremendous. Information and Communications Technology has helped to enhance and improve family relationship like everyone is now connected with the mobile phones, laptops, palmtops, viral conferencing, etc. but some of them believe that Information and Communications Technology has separated family and friends with each other.

Information and Communications Technology has allowed new friendship and relationships in virtual communities, and it is important to know that such relationships are genuine. This technology has brought new and different jobs over the internet, but these changes and opportunities are also endangered by problems of unemployment from computer replacing humans.

A wide range of new laws, regulations, rules, and practices are therefore needed if society is to manage these workplace and other changes and development brought about by Information and Communications Technology. Thus, the society need to consider the following ethical and social challenges related to Information and Communications Technology use:

- Recognition for personal and corporate ethics associated with

Information and Communications Technology.

- striking a balance between ethical, economic, and technological as well as political considerations.
- Intellectual property rights issue (trademarks, patents, copyright, and trade secrets).
- Non-violation of privacy and associated rights amidst electronic information data mining.
- The opportunity to commit crime with ICT (computer crime).
- Legal issues and limitations.
- Consequence of using ICT.
- Professional responsibilities (Kallman and Grillo, 1996).

Both individuals and organizations are using the information and communication technology which had major impacts on the society along with the use of its enabling technologies. Sometimes, IT experts don't able to find the solution, and they got confused that how to solve the queries of the users but they try to experiment and resolve it.

The persistent problems raised up by Information and communications technology contain the attack of individual and trade privacy, individual, and societal rights, intellectual property rights, values preservation and responsibility for the values and moments arising from the use of Information and communications technology, etc. There are issues that thrown up main challenges in the area of employment, working conditions and individuality. However, some areas still not have developed and require more progress associated with ICT.

IT plays an important role in various sectors like healthcare sector, finance, commerce, government, education, media, and entertainment and society at large. IT is one of the most challenging effects and can create some negative impacts on the society.

There are problems which has been raised, and it is linked with ethics. The problems can be harmful actions, personal privacy, and access right which are the part of the ethical issues.

IT Sector are allowing the data exchange and high level of information to other countries and different locations in the world and this problem needs to be solved because it is a case of personal privacy.

Sometimes, it is necessary to have the information as it will help the government in find the criminals and terrorists. The information should be used in a right way, and the information should not be shared with so many people. It has now become responsibility and challenge for everyone to maintain the privacy and integrity of data regarding individuals.

The authority should take control of the personal information of the individual, and nobody has the right to disclose any information without any reason. It is necessary to create PIN or password so that the information will not get disclosed.

Another problem which is a part of ethical issues is access right. The government has allowed to use the internet websites, but they are concerned with the untrusted applications which are still working in the internet as there are number of hackers who are involved in these things. They want to remove quickly and want to allow legal websites to the people.

In USA, the highly technological laboratories such as NASA and Los Alamos National Laboratories has tried to search different things and making people aware for the future. The computer hackers have tried to hack the information from the military computers and US government offices so that they have to increase their computer security and build new applications so that they find the hackers who are illegal doing the wrong things.

Loss of property, loss of information and property damage and unwanted environmental impacts are all become a part of computer ethics which is considered as negative consequences.

There can be an issue when the virus take place in the computer system. The virus can make harm to the important files which can also include the loss of data in the system. The important data stored in the system may be get destructed or lost. As a result, it becomes a challenge for the users to again recover the files which has lost as it requires efforts and time of the human being or IT experts. It becomes a challenge for the IT experts to protect the computer from viruses.

8.3.1. Plagiarism

Plagiarism can be defined as an amount of work which is copied from others, and the user submits the same work in its own way which it has copied. The individual follows the regular practice of copying the work which save the time and effort of the individual. This is considered as a highly unethical practice because the internet provides information of all types and it is easy to do.

Education: Education can be known for its online learning and students can use some tools to learn new things, but this can also distract them from studying because they also get some wastage materials on the internet. The Internet has had a variety of effects, some of which are quite disturbing.

Education is important in every aspects and computer play a major role in the education as it helps in developing the technical skills of the persons. The computer labs have increased in the schools, colleges, and universities for teaching more and more students. Teaching more students at one time can save efforts and time for the teachers, but they should make sure that they will teach with an interest. It has become important for the individuals to do work practically so that they will develop their skills which will help them in future.

Teachers also find it easy that the students prefer to research their papers with the help of internet rather than issuing book from library. In a related effect, the Internet has brought plagiarism into the computer era in two distinct senses.

The students may find simple and easy while working on the systems as they have electronic texts which they can copy and paste and it saves time of the individual.

There are lot of sources which are available in the internet so the students can just download the important papers which are used as a free source for the students. They don't need to go to purchase the papers as the papers are mainly available on the internet.

Teachers can mail the students easily, so the students get updated about all the things that have studied in the class or for future purposes. Teachers now have access to databases of electronically submitted papers and can easily compare their own students' papers against a vast archive of sources. Even a simple online search can sometimes find where one particularly well-turned phrase originally appeared.

8.3.2. Piracy

Piracy is a very serious problem, and it is considered as an illegal copying of software, and it is projected that approximately 50% of all programs on computer system are pirated copies. Programmers and the users of the system are used to protect the system from coding, and they spend hours in creating the programs by using elaborate code and surely need to be protected.

It is a global issue, as the big organization wants to earn more profits but if there is a problem that occur in the software can result in losing the job. As a result, it will have effect the company and damage profit margins.

File Sharing: It is very serious problem when there is transfer of files as the person might get some issue of transferring the file. The reason can be the changes in the software which are not allowing to share the files. There is one student in American college who invented Napster which is very useful tool for sharing the files, but other tools were also invented later to replace the Napster.

Napster is a tool that can be used for file-sharing system that allowed users to share electronic copies of music online. The recording companies are suffering with the use of this tool and losing revenues because one legal copy of a song was shared among many people.

P2P ("person-to-person") is a new tool that comes after the Napster which is also used for file-sharing because the record companies succeeded in shutting down Napster.

There is a problem with the Napster tool, but it has an alternative which is named as P2P tool. The P2P tool has become quite popular among the people. Earlier, P2P software has not been launched in the market as the industry not find it very useful, but they want to experiment with the tool, and later, it has been in a great demand because it has fast and easy process for transferring music files along with high-speed connections.

The P2P software makers must suffer, and they are getting loss that the official document owners have experienced, more-tricky schemes for avoiding anxiety and worry have been invented. The incapability to avoid file sharing has controlled the footage and movie industries to plan classy copy protection on their CDs and DVDs.

There are companies like Sony Corporation who introduces CDs into the market in 2005 but get into trouble because of copy protection that involved a special virus-like code that hid on a user's computer (Figure 8.1).

Figure 8.1: Piracy: a punishable offense.

Source: https://c1.staticflickr.com/4/3646/3558668316_0b9de4115b_b.jpg

8.3.3. Hacking

System Hacking is done by the person who have all kind of knowledge in the technical field. They can even break the passcode and can start the system. They can easily make a crime by doing things which are completely illegal. Earning money by hacking the system can be made easily as they can damage the systems or make a change in the system (Figure 8.2).

Figure 8.2: Computer hacker.

Source: https://www.maxpixel.net/Internet-Hacking-Hacker-Security-Cyber-Crime–2964100

The time has come to make the people aware that the system which they are using may be unsafe for them. They need to first check all the software's that whether they are working properly or not. The hackers can also help the people and organizations and save themselves against other hackers.

Hackers are the persons who requires lot of skills especially related to technology, and by checking the system, they can easily resolve the problem of the user. The users face lot of problems as the time of working in the deadlines, and it is important to have hackers on the backside. The hackers with this good skill can easily find that a system needs some improvement and it is insecure.

Hackers can play a main role for making the system or damaging the system. Many say that hacking capacity lead to some developments and improvements, but that it causes such a lot of disturbance that it is not value it in the future.

8.3.4. Computer Crime

Computer crime is the major issue for many countries. In many Countries, the personal data which is stored in the computer system has been stolen from somebody and leaked which is a crime. In 2006, the personal records of about 73 million people in the U.S. were accidentally lost, disclosed or stolen.

For Example, there is one case which has occurred in the country USA as there is some crime made by hacking the system where there is some personal information of the past members in the US military. According to the report, the data has been stolen, and the information is disclosed.

The government and security must be more careful and protect their systems from the thieves. There are number of people who have experience and high knowledge in the technical field. They can easily steal the information not only the person's information but credit card numbers and social security numbers. As a result, consumer may suffer losses because it has causes consumer fraud.

The government has provided the high security because the information is highly confidential. The government has also alerted the people as well as the companies to provide high security and protect the system.

Internet fraud takes many norms. It has become easy for the hackers to hack the system and disclose the information. Every government of the country has the information of everyone which has been stored in the system. The crime can be done in different ways such as fraud in credit card transactions, online banking transactions, and security systems.

Criminals of individuality robbery who had been caught reported the comfort with which they cashed in on taken information. There are many frauds which can be done through calling and electronic mail. The wrong information is provided to the customers through electronic mail to make money. The people send the schemes and do frauds to the customers.

There has been issue while using the internet as there may be lot of things which may be fake and people getting the wrong things to learn. The criminals can also transfer their money to their account by just having the debit card number of the other person. Every year, there has been a lot of losses to the customers which may be difficult to calculate.

Computer crime is also called as cybercrime, and there can be many different computer crimes like data stolen, sharing personal file which clearly poses ethical questions for society. Fraud and misuse are the acts that are illegal which is performed on computers.

There are various strategies which has applied in the system to avoid fraud. The person who is reaching to the website should verify their account; otherwise, the person also gets blocked from that website by making things changed.

8.3.5. Malicious Codes

Malicious code is the code causing damage to a computer or system as this code attacks several types of computer programs that were created with the purpose of causing data loss or damage. The three main types of malicious code attacks are viruses, Trojan horses, and worms.

A virus always attacks the system, and it is a malicious software that is attached to another program to execute an unwanted function on a workstation. An example is a program that is attached to command.com (the primary interpreter for Windows systems) and deletes certain files and infects any other versions of command.com that it can find.

A Trojan horse is a kind of program in the computer system that may change the settings of the computer system. Trojan horse virus can even attack the system, so there is a need for antivirus to protect from these attacks.

Viruses can even make the system slow, and it is very difficult for the users to work on the system. They can even damage the files which are unable to open. It can also cause various other problems in the system like there is problem to install the application or game applications. So, it is necessary to install a good anti-virus in the computer system and update whenever it is required.

Computer worms can also attack the system, and it may trouble the files. Upon positive misuse of the weakness, the worm copies its database from the offensive mass to the again broken system to start the series again.

Virus can affect the files, or anything related to personal data which can be lost easily. Once the virus enters into the system, all the things which are stored can be affected. The infection can then transfer itself to files and code on other computers through magnetic disks or other memory storage devices, computer networks, or online systems. The replicating viruses often multiply until they destroy data or render other program codes meaningless.

A virus can make the system restart again and again, and it is difficult for the user to make concentration on the work. The user will not be focused if they are getting trouble in the system. Virus takes very less time to make the system crash, and it can be more dangerous if the system will not be scanned from time to time.

Once the virus appeared in the system, it becomes very difficult for the user to work or store the data. Virus can appear anytime in the system as it not safe for the files which are stored. So, it is necessary to scan the virus; otherwise, the users must face serious consequences and cause systems to crash and organizations to cease operating for certain periods. The antivirus helps in making the system to work smoothly so that all the big businesses, as well as the organizations, have that antivirus which is installed in the system of every individual.

Logic bombs are also sometimes planted. There is clearly a lot of anti-virus software on the market now though that helps to deal with this ever-growing problem.

8.3.6. Ergonomics/Health Issues

The individual may suffer from various health issues. The health issues while using the computer can cause headache, arm or shoulder pain and it make stress on the eyes also. The individual can take some rest or break if they are sitting for a longer periods of time (Figure 8.3).

Figure 8.3: Health issues while using system.

Source: https://www.airforcemedicine.af.mil/MTF/Joint-Base-Lewis-Mc-Chord/News-Events/Article/1143698/mo-money-no-problem–62nd-cpts-keeps-finances-straight/

Nowadays, computers have become a need for everyone, but the workload can trouble the users. It has been noticed that the users are facing some health issues like eyestrain, back problems, eye infections and repetitive strain injury which are related to I.T.

The user should take care of their health as workload provide pressure and stress, so it is necessary to make the seat comfortable if the user is having problem. There are few organizations who will provide some exercise before starting the work and person feel fresh and relax.

8.4. ETHICAL ISSUES IN CYBERSPACE AND IT SOCIETY

8.4.1. International Efforts on Legislations

The government department are very much aware of their people, and existing laws are likely to be unenforceable against such crimes in many countries around the world. The growing threat to individuals is beginning to claim attention in national and international community. The limited amount of security from the legal aspect indicates that the organizations and the administrations should depend completely on the technologies available to them to guard themselves against the people who may spread incorrect information or the ones who handle the information in a very unhealthy and irresponsible way by either stealing it or destroying an important part of it

But this kind of approach is not adequate to make digital world a secure space to do business. The law and regulations must also be imposed and followed to ensure the safety. The nations that lack proper legal infrastructure against such unethical activities will eventually fall out of the path that leads them to grow into major economies.

As the rate of crime in the digital world rises and takes place across the world, the developed countries face the danger of getting the messages sent on the digital network blocked by the ones who take part in such misdeeds. The administrations in such nations much always keep an eye on the adequacy of their existing frameworks to combat these instances of crime. Until now, there only very few nations who have seriously taken up the topic and introduced legal regulations for the defaulters who commit such crimes.

The remaining nations should also start introducing the reforms in a legal framework on an urgent basis. It is very evident that a lot of hard work and efforts need to go in to ensure that there is no such incident of cybercrime taking place and that anyone involving themselves in such crimes must fear law so that they don't deal in any such activities.

8.4.2. Encryption Technology to Minimize Harmful Actions on Internet

During the time of World War II, it was very normal to use jumbled messages that were encrypted in secret patterns so that the enemy would not be able to interpret the messages even if they get hold of it in some way. Today on the Internet, these scrambled messages are quite popular for protecting and defending the credit card numbers and private information from enemy hackers. The mathematical method that is commonly found on the internet today that uses jumbling words to encode a message is known as 'encryption.'

Data can be converted in several forms such as e-mail, transactions, files, web information transmissions, etc. The encryption is generally used in internet shopping, stock trading, and online banking transactions, in ATMs and in and in electronic business-to-business transactions.

The data transmissions that happen on the homepage use a widely known method to encrypt the data in order to secure it, which is called Secure Sockets Layer (SSL). This kind of encryption is easy to be traced back to its source of the web page that begins with "https:" instead of the previously and commonly used "http." There is one more indication that informs about the use of SSL, in which there can be seen a gold lock on the status bar of the Web Browser.

Another indication is the golden outline that forms around the lock of the Security toolbar button. The most widely known methods to encrypt the important files and messages on the email are DES (Data Encryption Standard), RSA (Rivest Shamir and Adleman), and PGP (Pretty Good Privacy).

Each employee has a key method to encrypt data, which is required the use of two keys, a public, and a private key. The sender encrypts the email using the receiver's public key to encrypt an email message, which is widely known and can be obtained from an Internet public-key server or company. The email message is then sent in a locked, unreadable format.

In such a case the one who is receiving the message makes use of the key that they hold in private and which is a secret one, only used to decode the message. Some time ago, new Advanced Encryption Standard (AES) is a kind of security feature taken into consideration by the government of the United States. An encryption technique known as Rijndael is created by two coders from Belgium and is made in such a way that it proves to be a much safer option than the one that was being used earlier and can be operated on more than one hardware platform and in association with different software.

This method of coding makes use of very little memory and makes for the defensive mechanism against various kinds of attacks in the digital world. This kind of technique is quite significant, and it even grows more when the data goes through the systems that are shared or the networks that lack basic security features so as to provoke people to breach into the data networks illegally. In such cases the data which is in the category of being sensitive needs to be encrypted. One more kind of technique for encryption is known as "Digital ID."

Email is the method of exchanging messages between people using computers or electronic devices and people use this source to share some important information which can be confidential and important to another user and ensure that messages sent cannot be stopped and read by anyone other than the future receiver.

By using "digital IDs" in MS Outlook Express, senders can prove their identity in electronic transactions in a way like showing driver's license when people cash a check. Like encryption technique, digital ID is composed of a "public key," a "private key," and a "digital signature."

The techniques discussed above are used to transact data in private modes and in secrecy in order to disable people from indulging in unethical deeds. Moreover, these techniques may also be employed to avoid any unauthorized changes in the encrypted messages on the digital networks. There is one more kind of security system that is usually used to protect the computer networks known by the name of firewalls.

The firewall of the internet can be referred to as a system or more that commands the accessibility of information between the digital networks. The internet can be taken as a huge network of different digital networks that should be kept away from each other's territory.

This internet firewall provides help to fulfill two important functions. Firstly, it regulates the accessibility of the external networks to the internet systems. Secondly, it makes sure that only a controllable amount of information can be transmitted to the external world from the internal network. Thus, it contributes towards regulating and developing the policies for control of accessibility for the organizations.

Such strategies should address a growing number of worldwide community issues as these issues can be solved when the society provide people with jobs that are challenging, fulfilling, and interesting and the businesses and governments deal with possible exploitation of poor countries by wealthy countries and multinational conglomerates.

Many more ethical issues directly need the attention of governments, educational institutions, businesses, public, and private individuals worldwide. Strategies and Guidelines should be applied so that global information can be exploited in a socially and ethically sensitive way for future benefit and applications.

8.5. INTERNET REGULATION: NORMATIVE ISSUES

Many things which have been considered as illegal, in the other media, are illicit on the Internet also. A person cannot, for instance, release the secrets of state or trade on the Internet, and that too which usually is comprised of the defamation on another media platform, also performs it on the Internet.

This is that one regulation which is not independently meant for crimes related to internet, but are more focused towards those unethical issues which tries to get into the personal space of people which they are not willing to share with others (Figure 8.4).

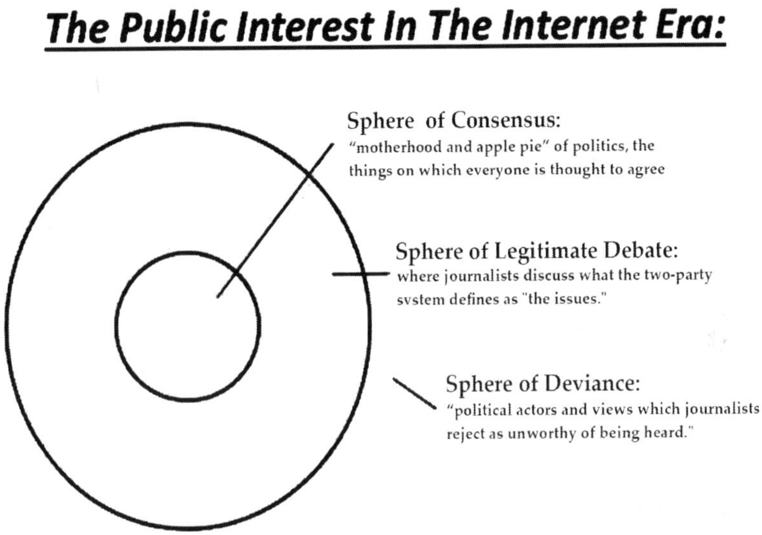

Figure 8.4: Normative theories.

Source: https://www.slideshare.net/nadianaseem5/normative-theories

In Australia, for example, defamation laws cover the Internet as well as other media, but there have been no objections to this. The regulation of primary concern in this chapter is that which attempts to restrict content or activity specifically on the Internet.

Thus, the question arises as to what if, similar to what has been suggested earlier, and the Internet is not actually a forum at all in the view that television is but more similar to that of a living space. Then, possibly, the question regarding the process of regulation is more related to the questions belonging to regulation in society in usual terms.

8.6. JOB DISPLACEMENT/WORK PRESSURES IMPOSED ON COMPUTER PROFESSIONALS

Nowadays, computer is used in every field whether it is business or an organization and it can be used on a large scale or small scale. The roles are quite different for each individual, and everyone has their own technique of using the computer. The work pressure may challenge the individuals as the organizations wants to know that whether individual can able to handle the tough situations or not.

On the other hand, many people are gaining the benefits of having more rewarding jobs, and they can write their skills on the job sites which helps in getting the suitable job related to his skills.

The growth of personal computing technology has transformed how people work and live in the 21st century. There is always have a challenge for the individuals as they keep on learning the new things and developing their skills. The technology keeps on changing and updating, so the experts try to give the knowledge to the large number of individuals.

There are many members in the company which are available in different field such as IT recruiters, middle-level managers and security consultants who try in helping the companies for achieving the goals and objectives.

Some of the major problems encountered by any IT professional in an office environment have been discussed below along with few important points which should be considered while addressing such issues:

8.6.1. Digital Divide

The digital divide poses a serious problem today. A new breed of haves' and 'have nots' are being created, between those that have access and can use a computer and the Internet, and those that do not have such access. There are clearly serious ethical implications here. Those that do not have such access may well be discriminated against, feel 'socially excluded' and miss out on many life opportunities.

Cloud Computing: Cloud Computing has raised many challenges for IT professionals as it also is having the ability to connect large numbers of computers on a single network. One of the spikiest issues is who owns the data and how the provider is supposed to keep it as it is an important concern in law implementation and litigation-related requests.

Debate also continues about whether companies are happier and comfortable by allowing their staff associated with IT can achieve the data or selling with a cloud seller who is especially specialized in safety procedures and rules affecting the average.

Cybersecurity: IT professionals are now taking as a challenge to develop new strategies against cybercrime because criminals need no special abilities to commit such crimes. People are so busy in managing things as the trend is changing continuously. There is always an update in the software as the technology keeps on changing.

There can be an issue with the system and every day there can be some problem which always occur in the system. The IT team is always available in the organization to solve the problems of the users. Sometimes, they are concerned with the new updates as some experts takes time to understand the problems of the individuals.

Remote Management: Conventional offices look not as much of appropriate when digital technologies, such as video conferencing, email, and instant messaging, enable employees to work remotely. As a result, IT professionals must face a lot of pressure to keep networks running at top capacity.

Everybody is responsible for their own work and IT experts have the big responsibility for providing the suitable systems to the individuals. They need to check the applications of the system before providing to the individual. IT managers more and more likely to troubleshoot difficulties at uncommon hours.

Talent Retention: It has been said that the IT jobs have a great demand in future and the Bureau of Labor Statistics estimates that demand for IT jobs will grow approximately 15 percent between 2012 and 2022. It is faster than the 11 percent estimated average for all other occupations. Request for specific areas like cyber security sparks severe order conflicts that favor the largest firms.

For example, Google raised managers' salaries by 10 percent to prevent defections to rivals like Facebook, "Forbes" magazine reported in June 2011. This trend leaves smaller firms struggling to recruit talent and industry leaders like Google continually replacing top performers who often jump ship for better offers.

New Technology: The technology is changing day by day and new technology advances quickly and shows up in media on all sides. This means that the competitors, managers at all levels and the users should pressure IT staff to implement new technology, simply because it is new.

The main challenge comes to the companies when there is a change in the technology. People are usually working on the old methods of techniques, and it takes time to better understand the new techniques. When there is a change in the technology, it takes time and effort to work on the more advanced level.

The companies set the goal to achieve more than the target to earn more profits. If the system should be able to work properly and smoothly than only the individuals will give the productivity and even more. This will give benefit to both the individuals as well as the organizations.

Big Data, cloud, mobility, and virtualization are now considered as a new technology in the IT sector, and these tools are mainly used experienced IT managers who understand their organization's priorities. Since every organization is different, the IT value of each new technology will vary with the organization's strategic goals.

8.6.2. In-House Cloud Plans

Many organizations can keep their data as well as applications in-house and manage everything themselves and yet to make cloud plans.

It is necessary to formulate the companies for a possible cloud move with the improvement and developments cloud computing technologies and to future-proof the network.

The main point is that to create portable applications today that will not hold the company back in the future, whatever that may hold.

To address this issue: The organization will make sure that the information will not leak. The low-level management will always take the permission from their managers to allow them to work from their home. The main advantage is that any change to a cloud-based solution needs to be done without using the new application.

8.6.3. Big Data Analytics

It has been expected while analyzing the data that it can raise by 800 percent after the five years. The biggest challenge for the IT experts is that there are more than 80 percent of data which seems to be free. Unstructured data varies in its formats, including email, formatted document, plain text, blog, animation, standard, and non-standard image, video, voice, sensor input, and web search logs. Structured data is slower than unstructured data.

As a comparatively new and untouched source of structural and organizational understanding, unstructured data analytics are likely to expose more important data and information about interrelationships that were formerly very hard and difficult to determine. Part of that unstructured data contains data from societies, communities, groups, and social networks external the organization which is known as "the collective."

To address this issue: The massive amount and growth of unstructured data rapidly outpaces traditional solutions and calls for new volume handling. Big Data analytics needs new methods for storing, taking, and evaluating the data in order to offer best deals to the organization.

Data is generated in real time, and the demands call for useful information to be ready as needed. Solutions like 100 GB Ethernet, parallel- processing, and SSDs (Solid State Drives) offer good response times. The data should be collected from different sources for analyzing and capturing the big and suitable data which is the main responsibility for the organization. The organization needs to know the nature and value of the big data so that they can achieve the organizational goals.

8.6.4. Virtualization

Virtualization remains to increase from desktops to servers to switches, routers, and firewalls. Today, Virtualization is used so that it has a strong control over these devices and it can be applied to a wide range of system layers. In fact, the infrastructure of the organizations needs high servers as it can be provided with the license.

These tasks need to be extended into the virtualized environment, as well as integrated with the existing workflow and management processes. It can be also be used in defining the hard drive as well as defining the hardware.

8.6.5. BYOD and BYOA

The main plan of IT sector is to maintain control as it has controlled user's devices. The Chief Information Officer and IT managers of the company has decided to secure: the network infrastructure or the organization's data. When a user brings their own device, they will also bring their own applications (BYOA) that they have been accustomed to. That is a plus for productivity and a challenge for IT security.

Many individuals will store their data in the mobile device for the backup if they lose the data from the system. It can be done by copying the files to the folders if there can be a data loss so that the individual can restore them easily. The individuals may have a data back plan if they have face issue in documents, personal files, music, picture files, emails, etc.

Shadow IT: IT Team and IT Experts are the backbone of the IT industry, and the data can be changed daily. Even the individuals have the responsibility to make the habit of running certain backups, and it should follow the best practice for storing backups because there can be a damage in the servers.

There are many other departments like marketing, sales, accounting, etc. which are considering independent arrangements with outside IT service providers.

8.6.6. Boomers

The organization arrive with different skill sets and new ways of looking at and using technology. The entry-level candidates entering the workforce are often much more loyal to themselves, what they know and, in some cases, to their peers than they are to the organization.

8.6.7. Interoperability

Customers and Users are more demanding of the products on their mobile devices and desktops. It all comes down to communicating effectively with one another. Systems need to send and receive data that will be well-suited on all user platforms.

Open standard is a standard that has various rights on the systems, and it usually work on the system applications. It has no single definition, but it is used for data exchange among different services and products.

Individuals who are working at the basic level can perform and interact easily with many other systems. Designers must avoid exclusive planning and use only open planning and backgrounds.

8.6.8. User Systems

Laptops, Desktops, notebooks, tablets, and smartphones are already an integral part of many user's lives. The person can use any of these electronic devices for work. There has been an alternative as the users can use their smartphones and tablets which is also helpful in performing many tasks related to the system. Individual who are working in the system are connected to the internet, and the users are working on the multiple applications in the system. They can complete their work more quickly if the system is working smooth.

Energy Efficiency: According to the survey, it has estimated that a twenty-five-thousand-foot data center are able to use more than $4 million in energy about this year. Few Percent of data will be left, and that will be saved for future purposes, but it can affect the budget of the IT sector. Even the big organizations are developing some methods to improving the energy efficiency and energy monitoring.

The tools are easily available in a developing market for energy efficiency and monitoring. It has been observed that there are more than 25 merchants who have entered this market. These tools display consumption at the application level and sometimes on the expedient level.

Creating Value: IT sector will face an issue regularly in case of value creation. The department which are related to the IT can provide and increase the number of systems. There can be no shortage of the systems in the organization departments. IT managers can also forward the list to the IT departments to improve their non-working systems.

The creation value is done to maintain hardware or software, small or mid-sized firms that can easily depend on the cloud for standardized services. That means a different way of outsourcing non-core activities to keep the focus on value creation.

8.6.9. Social Networks

Social networks like Facebook, Twitter, youtube, and LinkedIn have different ways to connect through the people. Customers, suppliers, and others are currently talking about every organization on some form of social media.

There are many departments like Marketing department, IT department, Healthcare department which need to make discussions and show their presence in the conservations. Semantic analysis tools can support the corporations mine that common discussion to figure new upgrades and products for improving the customer service, and support marketing and sales enterprises.

To address this issue: The main challenge in the market is that the customer should be satisfied with the quality of the products and services. As a result, it will give a strong platform for selling the goods and services and receive strong customer feedback (Figure 8.5).

Figure 8.5: Beware, what you share!!! Social Media; a platform provoking various unethical activities.

Source: https://media.defense.gov/2016/Sep/19/2001636674/–1/–1/0/160919-F-XX000–010.JPG

8.7. CHALLENGES AND ISSUES RELATED TO CYBERCRIME

Cybercrime series across a variety of activities. At one end are crimes that involve fundamental openings of personal or corporate privacy, such as attacks on the integrity of information held in numerical collections, stores, and the use of criminally gained digital information and data to blackmail a firm or individual.

Midway along the spectrum lie transaction-based crimes such as money laundering, fraud, trafficking in child pornography, digital piracy, money laundering, and counterfeiting. It is difficult to find the criminals who has done crime over the internet. The person who is expert or have knowledge in this field can only able check what has gone wrong.

8.7.1. Identity Theft and Invasion of Privacy

The Cybercrime is not only the crime of stealing the information and blackmailing, but it also affects both a real and a virtual body. Both the cases are different, and it has different consequences. For example, individuals do not have an official identity card but a Social Security number that has long served as a de facto identification number. The credit card which is stolen but the information can be used to recreate an individual's identity. Taxes are collected based on each citizen's Social Security number, and many private institutions to use the number to keep track of their students, employees, and patients. Access to an individual's Social Security number affords the opportunity to gather all the documents related to that person's citizenship—i.e., to steal his identity.

8.7.2. Internet Fraud

There are so many ways to make a fraud over the internet. The fraud can be done by sending the wrong emails or sending unnecessary emails like deposit money or security or transfer money to their account dealing them with multiple schemes. The fraud can also be done outside the country.

The message asks the receiver to cover about cost of affecting the assets and funds out of the country in return for getting a much more sum of money shortly (Figure 8.6).

Figure 8.6: Internet Fraud and its repercussions.

Source:https://cdn.pixabay.com/photo/2018/02/28/14/19/fraud-prevention–3188092_960_720.jpg

8.8. CONCLUSION

In the past, many individuals have face various IT challenges which has given a good learning to the customers, users, and even the departmental managers as they are ready for the challenges and work as a team to find the solutions and face the challenges related to the IT. This provides a light on the top that IT challenges facing today's information security professionals, and, hopefully, will provide IT and organizational management with some guidelines for prioritizing issues. Presenting them in this way may also show providers areas that they can help IT managers overcome these challenges.

REFERENCES

1. Globalknowledge.com., (n.d.). *Top 12 Challenges Facing IT Professionals (& How to Deal with Them) | Global Knowledge.* [online] Available at: https://www.globalknowledge.com/us-en/content/articles/12-challenges-facing-it-professionals/ [Accessed 14 Nov. 2018].
2. Gunarto, H., (n.d.). *Ethical Issues in Cyberspace and IT Society*, p. 8.
3. Heibutzki, R., (n.d.). *Challenges of Information Technology Management in the 21st Century*. [online] Work.chron.com. Available at: https://work.chron.com/challenges-information-technology-management–21st-century–28780.html [Accessed 14 Nov. 2018].
4. Norton, A., (2011). *News, Tips, and Advice for Technology Professionals – Tech Republic*. [online] Tech Republic. Available at: https://www.techrepublic.com/blog/10-things/10-challenges-facing-it/ [Accessed 14 Nov. 2018].
5. Ugbogbo, S., (n.d.). *Ethical Issues in Information Technology- A Conceptual Approach* (p. 20). [eBook]. Available at: https://www.iuokada.edu.ng/journals/5B6AA29B40ADBA7.pdf [Accessed 14 Nov. 2018].
6. Kallman, E. and Grillo, J. (1996). Ethical decision making and information technology. Boston: McGraw-Hill.

INDEX

M

N

O

P

Q

R

S

T